THE   FRAGILE   "WE"

Northwestern University
Studies in Phenomenology
and
Existential Philosophy

THE
FRAGILE "WE"

Ethical Implications
of Heidegger's
Being and Time

Lawrence Vogel

Northwestern University Press
Evanston, Illinois

1994

Northwestern University Press
Evanston, Illinois 60208-4210

Copyright © 1994 by Lawrence Vogel. Published 1994 by Northwestern University Press. All rights reserved.

ISBN   0-8101-1139-X (cloth)
ISBN   0-8101-1140-3 (paper)

Printed in the United States of America

Library of Congress Cataloging-in-Publication Data

Vogel, Lawrence.
     The fragile "we": ethical implications of Heidegger's Being and
     Time / Lawrence Vogel.
          p.   cm. — (Northwestern University studies in phenomenology &
     existential philosophy)
          Includes bibliographical references and index.
          ISBN 0-8101-1139-X (alk. paper). — ISBN 0-8101-1140-3 (pbk. :
     alk. paper)
          1. Heidegger, Martin, 1889–1976. Sein und Zeit. 2. Heidegger,
     Martin, 1889–1976—Ethics. 3. Ethics, Modern—20th century.
     4. Ethics, German—History—20th century. I. Title. II. Series.
     B3279.H48S489 1994
     111—dc20   94–13274
                                                                       CIP

Contents

CONTENTS

Acknowledgments

In the beginning there is gratitude, for the beginning is written at the end of a long journey that could never have been completed without different kinds of support from many fellow-travelers.

It is rare that one gets introduced to philosophy by teachers as dedicated and inspiring as those at Vassar College, and rarer still that one has the opportunity to begin one's career as a colleague of one's former teachers. I feel doubly lucky. They profess and exemplify the idea that the life of philosophy is conversation. My special appreciation on innumerable levels goes to Mitch Miller, Michael McCarthy, Michael Murray, and Jesse Kalin. I also feel grateful for the students I taught at Vassar. Seminars with them stimulated most of the thought behind this project.

At Yale Karsten Harries teaches about Heidegger with the same care and clarity that inform his writing. It was an honor to study with one who set the standard for research in the area, and a stroke of good fortune to have an adviser who read one's work diligently and thoughtfully, and who knew when to say "Stop" and when to say "Run."

Conversations with many friends—once centered in New Haven, but now dispersed—have kept philosophy alive. Special thanks go to Bob Gooding-Williams and Louis Goldring for fifteen years of to-and-fro; also to Alan Wright, Judith Butler, Lorenzo Simpson, Ian Shapiro, Paul Stern, Georgia Warnke, and the Ponet family. Judith—whose own life is a model of serious thought—was instrumental in helping my manuscript get a reading; so to her I am especially grateful.

Much philosophy happened in my conversations with my "non-philosopher" friends, Chuck Burbridge and Doug Nygren. Doug patiently helped me to see that you can't fly a kite with weights on the tail.

My current colleagues at Connecticut College have provided an environment of unqualified support for my interests. Special thanks to Mel Woody and Julie Rivkin for encouraging me to let go of the manuscript at last—and, of course, to the editorial group at the Northwestern

University Press, especially Susan Harris, for so generously shepherding the project to its completion.

The longest debt goes to my parents, Naomi and Walter, and my sister, Lisa, for not only accepting, but loving one who pursues the strange path of philosophy.

Last but foremost, words can't capture what I owe to my wife, Carol Freedman, master of the delicate balance between aspiration and acceptance. To be lucky enough to travel with her through life is to be on a deep journey. I vow to be as good to her as she completes her first book as she has been to me in the completion of this one.

Introduction:
Fundamental Ontology as a
"Fundamental Ethics"

I

In his "Letter on Humanism" Martin Heidegger claims that the fundamental *ontology* he works out in *Being and Time* offers a "fundamental
ethics."[1] And despite his insistence in *Being and Time* itself that fundamental ontology only *describes* the essential structures of human existence, the distinction between authenticity and inauthenticity surely carries *prescriptive* weight. At stake in the distinction is nothing less than the
alternatives of either "winning oneself" or "losing oneself."[2] Furthermore, Heidegger admits that authenticity is a "factical *ideal*" that governs
the entire account of Being-in-the-world (*SZ*, 310). If *Being and Time*
appears to lay the foundation for the imperative, "Dasein ought to be
authentic," the reader wonders what sort of character-ideal its hero, the
authentic individual, represents.

But if "anticipatory resoluteness"—the posture toward life that Heidegger calls "authentic"—is akin to the life-affirming honesty of Nietzsche's "Overman" who stands "beyond good and evil," then the "ought"
at the basis of the prescription, "Be authentic," does not establish a *moral*
imperative. Fundamental ontology might be a "fundamental ethics"
without having anything to do with what we ordinarily call "morality." In
fact Heidegger states that fundamental ontology does not have moral
content but only lays down "the existential conditions for the possibility
of any morality whatsoever" (*SZ*, 286).

The impression that one looks in vain for an account of morality
in the "fundamental ethics" of *Being and Time* is reinforced by Heidegger's denial that authenticity tells us precisely who we ought to be or
what we ought to do. A moral code or principle would alleviate the anxiety one feels in becoming aware that one's possibilities are not grounded in any absolute, nonhistorical foundation. Heidegger states explicitly
that the *existential* meanings of guilt, conscience, and responsibility are
"perverted" by the commonsense, *moral* interpretation of these phenom-

ena (*SZ*, 281). Existential guilt—the demand that one take responsibility for one's situation even though one did not create it in the first place—is more basic than moral guilt. And the call of existential conscience summoning one to existential guilt does not speak with the impersonal, and so reassuring, voice of morality: "Do what *anyone* in your shoes ought to do." Rather it addresses the individual personally: beckoning one to recollect not universal guidelines but one's particular, "ownmost" possibilities. Perhaps what Heidegger means by "the silent call of conscience" is best captured by a Hasidic tale related by Martin Buber.

> "When I get to heaven," said the Hasidic rabbi Susya shortly before his death, "they will not ask me, 'Why were you not Moses?' but 'Why were you not Susya?'"[3]

But in Buber's philosophy responsibility for myself always occurs within the horizon of responsibility to the "Thou." In Heidegger's account of existence, on the other hand, the self appears to take priority over others. Buber criticizes Heidegger for offering an egocentric and "monological" variant of Kierkegaardian existentialism.

> Heidegger secularizes the Single One of Kierkegaard; that is, he severs the relation to the Absolute *for* which Kierkegaard's man becomes a Single One. And he does not replace this "for" with any worldly and human "for."[4]

If choices are not grounded in a source that would provide their measure—if norms only derive their authority from the free wills of individuals or the conventions of historical peoples who acknowledge and appropriate them—then it appears that freedom is the "groundless ground" of human ideals. But a freedom that knows no measure seems indistinguishable from spontaneity or arbitrary commitment.

Reading Heidegger against the background of Kant and Kierkegaard, one is inclined to interpret authenticity as an annihilation of both (1) the moral limits immanent in the Kantian "autonomous self" who is governed by the categorical imperative, and also (2) the religious limits deriving from the Infinite for the sake of which Kierkegaard's "knight of faith" is commanded to suspend the moral law. For Heidegger's authentic individual, anxiety does not arise—as it does for the "knight of faith"—from the conflict between moral and religious absolutes, but rather from the experience of the absence of any absolutes orienting one's existence. To be authentic is to open up to the absence of any universal, nonhistorical directive governing who one ought to be. Authenticity appears to imply moral subjectivism or relativism.

But what do we have a right to expect from an ontology that would disclose the "fundamental ethical" character of existence? If we demand too much determinacy from such an ethics, we cannot but expect a projection of a particular, provincial form of life masquerading as the universal. Yet if we demand too little, we are left with an ethics that fails to assist us when we face concrete issues: that fails even to show how we are always already oriented toward a sphere of judgments and predisposed to recognize the moral goodness or evil, rightness or wrongness, justice or injustice, of certain possibilities. We should be suspicious of an analysis of human existence that relegates the moral domain as a whole to the level of inauthenticity, interprets self-responsibility as a process wholly independent of the claims of moral responsibility, and fails to account for the prior determination of the individual's freedom within a range of moral considerations she does not constitute but by which she finds herself obligated. One critic, Stanley Rosen, asserts, "Heidègger's method . . . fails to capture the living nutrient of human existence: *phronesis*. Heidegger cannot distinguish, as we do in everyday life, between a good and a bad man."[5] The difficulty, of course, is to avoid projecting one's own moral prejudices into one's image of the essence of human existence. It remains to be seen whether fundamental ontology possesses a moral depth that is missing on the surface of its structures.

The problem of the ethical significance of *Being and Time* is all the more perplexing and pressing in view of Heidegger's own behavior during the Third Reich, his silence for two decades after it, his evasive responses to interlocutors' specific questions in the notorious *Der Spiegel* interview of 1966, and the deceptions evident in his posthumously published account of the times. That Heidegger leaps over concrete concerns about the oppression and suffering of individual human beings, never explicitly mentions the Final Solution, and clearly feels more comfortable when he shifts the discussion to more ambiguous epochal developments only aggravates the worry that his "fundamental ethics" is too indeterminate to guide judgment—or, worse yet, that it is susceptible to chauvinistic appeals. It is important, of course, to be careful that the philosophical and the biographical not be confused: that it not be assumed that Heidegger's comportment represents or follows from the ethical substance of his thought. But one can be too careful. A close reading of his "Rectoral Address" and official speeches during 1933–34 shows that Heidegger couches his enthusiastic, even if critical, support for Nazism in the discourse of authenticity elaborated in *Being and Time*. Is the portrayal of existence offered by fundamental ontology so lacking in moral fiber that the affirmation of Nazi ideology by a cultured German in 1933 could qualify as an authentic appropriation of his heritage? One worries that Heidegger's "fundamental ethics" is so morally empty or corrupt that it cannot help one to identify and condemn even the clearest cases of evil.

II

Heidegger gives us a clue as to what he means by "ethics" in his "Letter on Humanism," where he traces the term to the Greek notion of *ethos* whose primary meaning he interprets as "abode" or "dwelling-place." Fundamental ontology is an ethics in that the analysis of Being-in-the-world articulates what it means to dwell on the earth as a mortal. Inauthenticity describes a way of dwelling in which one has chosen to avoid facing the structure of one's existence as a whole—a structure bounded by one's Being-unto-death. Inauthentic Dasein loses itself by becoming absorbed in the anonymity of everyday life. One who dwells authentically, by contrast, stands open to the structure of existence and takes hold of his situation in light of the constraints of history, embodiment, and mortality.

From a properly "ethical" point-of-view, the importance of fundamental ontology for our epoch is that it offers an antidote to what Heidegger comes to see as the prevailing *ethos* of modernity: an *ethos* defined by the "world-picture" of mathematical physics initiated by "the Copernican revolution."[6] This picture, whose ontological presuppositions are elaborated by Descartes, has us lost in infinite, homogeneous space in a nature governed not by rational necessity or divine providence but by sheer chance. This universe is no longer the living, harmonious, hierarchical, teleological *cosmos* or "chain of Being" conceptualized in Greek contemplation, nor is it the sacred order of creation open to Jewish or Christian faith. Moderns repudiate classical cosmology's understanding of art (*techne*) as humanity's completion of nature (*physis*) and also reject medieval theology's reading of nature as an artifact of the supernatural artist. If the universe is neither eternal and divine (Athens) nor contingent and created (Jerusalem), then humanity has no definite place in the hierarchy of an eternal or created *cosmos*.

When early modern poets and philosophers register despair over how the new science displaces humanity, they presume that "the death of God" leaves us without our bearings: that without a foundation and a center our dwelling loses its meaning. In his "Anatomy of the World" (1611) the metaphysical poet, John Donne, writes of humankind's need to find "a new compass for their way":

> And new philosophy calls all in doubt,
> The element of fire is quite put out;
> The sun is lost, and th' earth, and no man's wit
> Can well direct him where to look for it.
> And freely man confesse that his world's spent
> When in the Planets and the Firmament
> They seeke so many new; and see that this
> Is crumbled out againe to his Atomies.
> 'Tis all in pieces, all cohaerence gone;
> All just supply, and all Relation:
> Prince, Subject, Father, Sonne, are things forgot,
> For every man alone thinkes he hath got
> To be a Phoenix, and that then can bee
> None of the kinde, of which he is, but hee.
> This is the world's condition now.

Pascal, too, poignantly voices the sense of physical and metaphysical homelessness arising from the new science:

> When I consider the short duration of my life, swallowed up in the eter-
> nity before and after, the little space which I fill . . . , cast into the infi-
> nite immensity of spaces of which I am ignorant and which know me
> not, I am frightened, and shocked at being here rather than there; for
> there is no reason why here rather than there, why now rather than
> then. Who has put me here? By whose order and direction have this
> place and time been allotted to me?[7]

The pursuit of truth in modern natural science is "unethical" in the sense that it denies us a sense of belonging to or of being at home in a larger natural order—because a universe of material objects interpret- ed as *res extensa* has no place for meaning and value. When we conceive of ourselves essentially in terms of our power to think "objectively," we feel homeless, displaced, and only contingently related to others and things. Heidegger traces the uprootedness of modern humanity to a philosophical source: the Cartesian picture in which we are "worldless" subjects capable of knowing the material universe by virtue of our ability to rise above prejudices imposed by the constraints of embodiment, ordinary language, and history.

Heidegger does not reject the natural scientific attitude, however, but shows its dependence on our more primordial participation in an everyday, historical world: a social environment that is always already a context of meaning. Unlike Kant, who sought to show the limits of knowledge in order to make room for faith, Heidegger seeks to show the limited and derivative place of theoretical knowledge within the meaningful field of our everyday "care": our "concern" with things and "solicitude" toward others. The universe as modern science presents it is a reduced version of how the world is from the perspective of our pragmatic, moral, and aesthetic interests. It is only natural that we feel lost in space as it is conceptualized by mathematical physics, for this is not the place wherein we dwell. The human image derived from the Copernican-Galilean interpretation of nature is untenable because science's posture of objectivity is simply closed off to the world we live in. In and of itself, natural science does not deprive us of our *ethos*. It only appears to do so when we assume that its method for knowing how things are is primary and that our self-interpretation should be based on it.

Being and Time is a response to metaphysical nihilism or "the death of God": the historical situation in which humanity experiences the absence of an ahistorical background-order securing its place within a meaningful whole. But fundamental ontology articulates what it means to dwell from within this nihilism, not by way of a nostalgic return to classical cosmology or medieval theology. In describing Being-in-the-world Heidegger delineates our *ethos* or dwelling-place without grounding it in a "higher" order governed by natural or divine ends. Though the temporal structure of human existence—Being-unto-death and historicality—remains the same for all persons, the content and actual possibilities that one is called on to appropriate depend on one's particular cultural and historical circumstances. Fundamental ontology is a fundamental ethics insofar as it reminds us of the worldly dwelling-place we always already inhabit even in the absence of any cosmic place. It allows one to affirm *metaphysical* nihilism—the loss of an "onto-theological" foundation—without seeing in this destiny a reason for despair. Rather than plunging us into a mood in which nothing matters or anything goes, the anxiety-provoking idea that "No-thing" grounds our Being-in-the-world simply returns us to our care for our own Being as the basis on which anything can matter to us.

III

But this does not suffice to allay worries about *moral* nihilism. How, one might ask, does the way that I care for *my own* Being bear on my caring for the Being of *others?* Ever since the publication of *Being and Time* in 1927, many of Heidegger's most astute critics, including Buber, Löwith, Levinas, Jonas, Fackenheim, Theunissen, and Tugendhat, have charged that his account of authenticity is morally nihilistic because it fails to do justice to the social dimension of human life. It cannot explain how the very existence of other persons imposes restraints on how one may right-fully exercise one's freedom, and so it cannot ground even the most basic of all taboos: the prohibition against murder. Time and again it has been asserted that Heidegger's fundamental ontology is either egocen-tric or chauvinistic. It is especially important to assess the validity of these charges because many see Heidegger's turn to Nazism in 1933 as follow-ing logically from an indifference, and even hostility, to "otherness" in the premises of his early philosophy.

In the chapters that follow I present three interpretations of authentic existence—the existentialist, the historicist, and the cos-mopolitan—each of which is a plausible version of the personal ideal depicted in *Being and Time.* By describing each version as "plausible" I do not mean that Heidegger might equally have intended any of the three: only that a thoughtful reading of the text might yield each interpreta-tion. The evidence—especially his remark to Karl Löwith that his con-cept of "historicity" formed the basis of his partisanship for National Socialism—indicates that Heidegger favored what I am calling the his-toricist interpretation of authenticity. But a text cannot be reduced to an author's intentions. In spite of Heidegger's disclaimers there are reasons why *Being and Time* gets read so often as a manifesto of existentialism.

I claim that only the cosmopolitan interpretation is able to defend fundamental ontology against the charge of moral nihilism. Yet I admit that the cosmopolitan reading does not faithfully represent Hei-degger's intentions and, furthermore, requires a supplementation of his analysis in several respects. It requires, first, that Heidegger's inadequate treatment of Being-with-Others be developed and, second, that moral conscience be given a more prominent role in the structure of human existence than Heidegger accords to it. My favored interpretation of authenticity demands that certain underplayed strains in *Being and Time* be accented and turned against the more dominant voices of the text.

In chapter 1, I prepare for my three readings of the meaning of authenticity by discussing Heidegger's account of inauthentic existence.

Of particular concern is why Heidegger explicitly relegates morality to the domain of the inauthentic. This fact alone should make one suspicious of any attempt to interpret authenticity along moral lines. I shall claim, however, that Heidegger's demotion of morality is a critique of a deficient and derivative conception of morality, not of morality *as such*. Perhaps a richer and more fundamental sense of morality can find a grounding in Heidegger's conception of authenticity after all.

On the "existentialist" reading, presented in chapter 2, the authentic individual is free to "create his own values" independent of the impersonal expectations of public opinion and even moral principle. This image of what it means to be self-responsible raises the specter of "subjectivism": that nothing is impermissible except for what the individual decides to define as such. This reading takes its bearing from Heidegger's death-analysis which does give the impression that the authentically free individual is a solitary, private hero who makes his own decisions without regard for the demands of a larger public order. But the primacy of the death-analysis, and so of this individualistic conception of authenticity, is called into question in Heidegger's discussion of "historicality," where the individual is placed in the context of a larger community with its own traditions and destiny.

On the "historicist" interpretation, offered in chapter 3, authenticity does not involve the individual creating values *ex nihilo*, for it requires the creative appropriation of one's "tradition": where "tradition" means the historically rooted, communal constraints that inevitably condition one's possibilities. The authentically historical individual never chooses in a vacuum but always repeats culturally specific possibilities embodied in the life of a precursor or "hero." Much of the rhetoric in Heidegger's discussion of the historical dimension of existence foreshadows the discourse we find six years later in his "Rectoral Address" and pro-Nazi speeches. This provokes worries about chauvinism and, more broadly, "relativism": for if one's choice of self is governed by the authority of tradition, then there seems to be no standpoint from which one can criticize the prejudices of one's group. Nothing precludes one's authentically making commitments that are hostile to the most basic interests of some members of one's own community or of violating the dignity of outsiders.

But it is not clear that Heidegger's emphasis on persons' historical and cultural rootedness implies that, in the words of Emmanuel Levinas, fundamental ontology "murders" the other or the stranger. In spite of Heidegger's thin treatment of Being-with-Others, he does state that an authentic self-relation alters the way one is able to encounter other

persons. Authenticity makes possible "liberating solicitude": an orientation in which one is able "to become the conscience of Others" by "letting them be free for their own possibilities." But what are the moral
implications of the authentic individual's ability to adopt this "liberating" posture toward others? Heidegger's official position is that liberating solicitude is an ontological, not a moral, category. I explore whether
it is possible that an ontological category here makes a moral difference.
On the "cosmopolitan" interpretation, presented in chapter 4, authentic
self-responsibility implies neither "subjectivism" nor "relativism," for it
makes possible "authentic Being-with-Others": a posture in which one
feels an obligation to respect the dignity of other persons and compassion for the suffering of others. Recall, however, that this interpretation
requires a creative supplementation of Heidegger's text at odds with the
author's intentions.

In the concluding discussion, chapter 5, I develop some parallels
between my three interpretations of the moral status of *Being and Time*
and three moments in the contemporary debate between liberal and
communitarian political thinkers over the proper way of construing the
relationship between the individual and society. In particular, I show
how the problem of defending cosmopolitan ideals within the context of
Heidegger's historicism parallels the problem of justifying liberal ideals
within the framework of communitarianism. I think it is plausible, given
my amendments to fundamental ontology, to interpret it as providing an
existential basis for the second version of Kant's categorical imperative:
always treat other persons as ends-in-themselves, never solely as means.
Ultimately I try to square this apparently transhistorical and foundational principle with the claims that fundamental ontology implies (1) historicism and (2) antifoundationalism.

IV

Given "the Heidegger controversy" that rages today, and because I am a
Jew, it is somewhat embarassing to be defending Heidegger's project
against its accusers. But in defending a version of Heidegger's *project* I do
not purport to be coming to the defense of *Heidegger* either as a man or
as the exponent of a moral position. I have no admiration for Heidegger's moral character. And I recognize the connections between his early
philosophy and his attraction to Nazism. But just as there is a danger in
becoming an apologetic or obscurantist disciple of a thinker—a danger

to which too many "Heideggerians" have succumbed—so there is the equally unfortunate prospect that the promise of someone's thought will be disregarded because his character turns out to be disappointing. No less a critic of Heidegger's than Jürgen Habermas has recently reminded us that

> the Heideggerian oeuvre, especially the thought in *Being and Time*, has attained a position of such eminence among the philosophical ideas of our century that it is simply foolish to think that the substance of the work could be discredited, more than five decades later, by political assessments of Heidegger's fascist commitments. . . . With *Being and Time* Heidegger proved himself, almost overnight, to be a thinker of the first rank. . . . From today's standpoint, [his] new beginning still presents the most profound turning-point in German philosophy since Hegel.[8]

The cosmopolitan interpretation of fundamental ontology that I recommend as an antidote to moral nihilism runs counter to Heidegger's own anticosmopolitan convictions. But it does draw out some underdeveloped themes in Heidegger's explicit project that let one reinterpret that project against Heidegger's intentions. I hope that this contributes both to a diagnosis of what there is about *Being and Time* that invites moral nihilism, and to a sense of how fundamental ontology might be recast so that "the other" is accorded the place she deserves in an account of human existence.

1

Heidegger's Critique of Morality: The Inauthenticity of the Morally Conscientious Individual

I

The common view that Heidegger's authentic individual is a spiritual descendent of Nietzsche's "Overman" gains plausibility from the fact that *Being and Time* officially locates morality in the domain of inauthenticity. To assess the view that authenticity is a morally nihilistic ideal we must understand the ambiguous role that morality actually plays in Heidegger's account of existence.

Heidegger calls the existing person "Dasein" or "Being-in-the-world" because we are not primarily subjects "in here" who experience ourselves as standing over against objects "out there," but beings who initially understand ourselves from the things and others with which we are involved in a practical situation into which we have been thrown. The "objective" dimension is not projected forth from some inner sphere of worldless subjectivity; rather, the world is thrown beforehand as the a priori of Being-in-the-world: as the place where Dasein finds itself participating "in the swim of things."

Things are there for us first and foremost not as "present-at-hand" objects to be known but as "ready-to-hand" equipment to be used. And the world presents itself not as the super-object containing all objects but as the functional environment that grants things their place within a meaningful network of relations. In its everyday business Dasein encounters other persons as a matter of course because the equipment with which one is "concerned" refers immediately to a "with-world" of producers, consumers, and owners with whom Dasein deals in "solicitude." As Dasein gives itself over passionately to the world its primary mode of self-reflection is not an explicit act of self-apprehension but the self-disclosure already in play precisely when Dasein is absorbed in its everyday projects.

For the most part Dasein does not distinguish itself from "the Others"; it is, like them, immersed in average possibilities prescribed by prevailing social practices, norms, and modes of interpretation.

> The Self of everyday Dasein is *the Anyone*, which we distinguish from the *authentic Self*—that is, from the Self which has been taken hold of in its own way. Dasein has been *dispersed* into "the Anyone," and must first find itself. This dispersal characterizes the "subject" of that kind of Being which we know as concernful absorption in the world we encounter as closest to us. If Dasein is familiar with itself as "the Anyone," this means at the same time that "the Anyone" itself prescribes the way of interpreting the world and Being-in-the-world which lies closest. Dasein is for the sake of "the Anyone" in an everyday manner, and "the Anyone" itself articulates the referential context of significance. (SZ, 129)

Heidegger calls Dasein's tendency to lose itself in the public, workaday world its "falling." But Dasein does not fall into the world from some "purer and higher 'primal status'" (*SZ*, 176). Average everydayness is an *existentiale*, an essential and inescapable dimension of Dasein's existence. One never exists in a state of isolated purity apart from what "the Anyone" makes possible. Dasein is never a bare subject without a world nor an isolated "I" without others. "Authentically Being-one's-Self does not rest upon an exceptional condition of the subject, a condition that has been detached from 'the Anyone'; it is rather an *existentiell* modification of 'the Anyone'—of 'the Anyone' as an essential *existentiale*" (*SZ*, 130). There is no pure authenticity but at best an authentic appropriation of the inauthentic. The possibilities one can make one's own do not come from nowhere; they are handed down to one from the factical world to which one belongs. Though the extent of "the Anyone's" dominion changes through history, the fact of its dominion does not. It is ontological, not historical, and does not arise from external circumstances but from the heart of Dasein's existence.

Although he claims not to be waging any "moralizing critique of the everyday" (*SZ*, 167), Heidegger's portrait of everyday life surely has critical and moralistic overtones.[1] He describes persons as being primarily "inauthentic": "lost" in the public world into which they have "fallen," governed by the anonymous "Anyone" (*das Man*) to which each has ceded the burden of self-responsibility. While insisting that he does not mean to "disparage" the everyday (*SZ*, 167) or to evaluate it negatively (*SZ*, 175) he characterizes its mode of discourse as "idle talk" dominated by gossip, its mode of sight as "curiosity" marked by distraction, the lust for novelty and the refusal to dwell anywhere in particular, and its mode of interpretation as "ambiguity" or noncommittal superficiality. Being-in-the-world is essentially "tempting," "tranquilizing," "alienating," "entangled in itself," "turbulent," and "plunging downward." The person is faced with the value-laden alternatives of inauthentically "losing himself" in the possibilities prescribed for him by "the Anyone" or of authentically "winning himself" by diverting his attention from the leveling chatter of "the Anyone" and taking hold of his own possibilities (*SZ*, 42).

"Falling" is a pejorative term because it does not just characterize the way Dasein *happens* to be first of all and most of the time. Heidegger says that Dasein is motivated to *avoid* its "I-myself" by its wish to evade the anxiety that accompanies owning up to one's freedom. Dasein's tendency to define itself in terms of what a "normal" person in one's situation is expected to say and do arises from a *temptation* internal to Dasein's Being. Because it feels unsettling to face one's possibilities alone, to take one's own stand unsupported by the familiar context that usually guides one, Dasein tends to secure itself by losing itself in the anonymity of "the Anyone." "Everyone is the other, and no one is himself. '*The Anyone*,' which supplies the answer to the question of the '*who*' of everyday Dasein, is the '*nobody*' to whom every Dasein has already surrendered itself in Being-among-one-another" (*SZ*, 128). "The Anyone" is not definite "significant others" or a ruling class, but no one in particular: a nobody who manages nonetheless to exert an "inconspicuous domination" over the way Dasein lives. Absorption in what "the Anyone" is concerned with and conformity with what "the Anyone" expects disburdens one of the anxiety of self-responsibility.

Heidegger's portrayal of "the Anyone" finds its sociological complements in Charles Cooley's "looking-glass self," David Riesmann's "other-directed man," and Christopher Lasch's "narcissistic" personality, a recent fictional example of which is found in Woody Allen's *Zelig*.[2] What gives the illusion that such a person is not self-centered is that he seems to be so concerned about what others think. But this concern stems not from an interest in others for their own sake but from his need to reassure himself of his own secure place. His other-directedness is not the expression of altruism but of someone who depends too much on others' opinion of him. Consequently he tends to manipulate others to gain their approval or to alter his own self-presentation like a chameleon to fit in with his social surroundings. In this regard Heidegger sharply contrasts the solicitude between authentic Daseins who are secure enough in themselves "to let Others be free for their own possibilities" with interactions between inauthentic Daseins characterized by "ambiguous and jealous stipulations and talkative fraternizing in 'the Anyone' and what 'anyone' wants to undertake" (SZ, 298).

That everyday Mit-sein is ruled by gossip and jealousy—an interest in suppressing the exceptional and glossing over the subtle—implies that "the Anyone" is just as closed off from the authentic potentiality of other Daseins as it is from its own. The domination of oneself by "the Others" precludes an authentic relationship with others as other; one is unable to see beyond the shadow cast by "the Anyone." Since others are proximally those from whom Dasein does not distinguish itself, both Dasein and others get incorporated into "the Anyone." Others are encountered not for who they are in their own right but for what they do and what they are concerned with.

This is not to say that another Dasein is primarily a mere "It," some thing either ready-to-hand or present-at-hand, for the other remains a partner in solicitude, not an object of concern. In average everydayness, however, solicitude is not an authentic dialogue between individuals who confirm each other's independence but an absorption in worldly matters of common concern which "is tinged with distance, reserve and mistrust," even when it is cooperative and "one does the same thing as Others" (SZ, 122). Because everyday Mit-sein is based on a concealed "groundlessness" and suppressed anxiety, it is fraught with antagonism. "Under the mask of a 'for-one-another,' an 'against-one-another' is in play" (SZ, 175). Still, the antagonism remains mostly hidden by a veneer of cooperation.

II

It should surprise the reader, then, when Heidegger demotes morality tout court to the domain of "the Anyone" and asserts that our common-sense interpretation of guilt and conscience as moral phenomena is "inauthentically oriented" (*SZ*, 281). For it would seem that the morally conscientious individual is precisely one who is *not* lost in the crowd, who makes his own judgments and takes hold of his own possibilities in light of a higher standard than what "the Anyone" dictates. It would seem that authenticity gives birth to a sense of moral responsibility superior to whatever moral precepts reign in average everydayness: a higher conscience that may provide a check against the tendency of "the Anyone" to identify the right with the customary or the instrumental.

One might expect that Heidegger would identify authenticity with morally conscientious individuality or postconventional morality, and that this moral posture would provide a corrective for inauthentic selfhood and Being-with-Others alike. For it would seem that the morally conscientious individual lifts himself above the prevailing expectations of the group in order to do justice to other persons in light of a higher standard than what is publicly expected and respectable. He does not just drift along impelled by the social tides, but subjects his own prejudices and public opinion alike to critical scrutiny. It seems unfair to characterize the morally reflective individual as "losing himself in the talkative fraternizing and jealous and ambiguous stipulations of 'the Anyone' and what 'anyone' wants to undertake." The demands of moral conscience, of one's "better judgment," may call the individual to stand alone against public opinion in the name of what is truly best for the community.

Furthermore, if average everydayness involves a deficient kind of sociality, then authentic existence may open up the possibility, even the ideal, of authentic co-existence. And Heidegger confesses as much when he asserts: "When Dasein is resolute it can become the 'conscience' of Others. Only by authentically Being-their-Selves in resoluteness can people authentically be with one another" (*SZ*, 298). Authentic individuation, rather than isolating the person from others, opens him up to them in a new way and makes "liberating solicitude" possible: a relationship of "authentic care" in which one, on the basis of his resolute affirmation of his own existence, is able "to help the Other become transparent to himself *in* his care and to become free *for* it" (*SZ*, 122). Doesn't moral conscience not only separate that individual from "the Anyone" but also enable him to treat others as ends-in-themselves beyond the horizon of their public roles and stations? One anticipates that Heidegger's account of authentic existence will provide a moral foundation for criticizing the ways we treat each other in the average, everyday world.

Heidegger insists, however, that the experiences of moral guilt and conscience stem from one's having "fallen" into the public world dominated by "the Anyone." How are we to account for his puzzling claim that the morally conscientious individual exhibits "the essential *consciencelessness* within which alone the existentiell possibility of *being* 'good' subsists" (*SZ*, 288)? We must clarify why Heidegger takes moral conscience to be just another symptom of inauthenticity rather than an antidote to the ills of everyday *Mit-sein*.

At first it might seem that Heidegger slights morality because he identifies it with publicly prevailing customs and conventions. Primarily the normative is simply the normal. Doing the right thing means doing what "anyone" ought to do in similar circumstances according to what "the Anyone" expects of a respectable person. The standards for what counts as reasonable or responsible behavior derive initially from one's community. The morally upstanding individual in the everyday sense conforms to what "the Anyone" demands of a good person. The conformist is obviously inauthentic because he accepts without question the reigning public opinion about what is right. Normal morality, rather than placing the individual at a critical distance from the group, puts the stamp of approval on his going along with the crowd. It is surely true that much apparently moral behavior is motivated by a fear of punishment or a desire for approval. Yet if moral agency is understood in such restricted terms, then it is rooted in a flight from oneself into "the Anyone."

But this image of the morally conscientious individual is surely a caricature, and Heidegger is fully aware of this. Any behavior might be justified by an appeal to custom or convention because the moral content depends wholly on what "the Others" believe is right. Hannah Arendt has shown the danger of equating the conventional with the moral, the normal with the normative. Though it may happen that the conformist is generous and just, there is a deep connection between the thoughtlessness of "the Anyone" and what Arendt has called, in reference to Adolf Eichmann, "the banality of evil." She contends that the conditions of modern society in particular have invited evil on a monstrous scale rooted not in wickedness, pathology, or ideological conviction but in superficiality or the inability to think. There are more thoughtless than wicked people. And banality should be distinguished from stupidity, for many intelligent people remain thoughtless in the sense that they adapt themselves without much hesitation to sweeping changes in moral attitude and practice.

What is dangerous about such malleability is that moral content is irrelevant; what matters primarily is that there be some order to which one can conform. Those whose conscience is guided by prevailing social trends get accustomed to not making up their minds or thinking for themselves. They go whichever way the wind blows because they are more concerned with feeling comfortable than with the grounds of the principles they accept. In an epoch when people tend not to feel present to the eyes of God or even to their own better selves they take their bearings by going along with the faceless crowd. They are prepared to adapt even to radical reversals of content so long as a demagogue satisfies their fantasies of nostalgia or utopia or "law and order." Of the slide toward fascism, Arendt remarks that

> The faster men held to the old code the more eager they will be to assimilate themselves to the new one; the ease with which such reversals can take place under certain circumstances suggests indeed that everybody is asleep when they occur. This century has offered us some experience in such matters. How easy it was for totalitarian rulers to reverse the basic commandments of Western morality—"Thou shalt not kill" in the case of Hitler's Germany, "Thou shalt not bear false witness against thy neighbor" in the case of Stalin's Russia.[3]

Arendt does not suggest that thinking alone provides a panacea against evil; thinking has liabilities of its own, not the least of which is the threat of a licentiousness born of cynicism about the possibility of any secure standards. But there is some connection between the habit of critically distancing oneself from prevailing popular opinion and a level of moral conscientiousness that comes to more than obeying the voice of "the Anyone." Crucial to genuine moral conscience is the refusal to lose oneself in the anonymity of what "the Anyone" dictates, a willingness to take one's stand against what is fashionable, to criticize public opinion for the sake of the community, to judge what is right beyond the horizon of the taken-for-granted. That one think for oneself, of course, is no guarantee that one's judgments will be wise. If not thinking can lead to great evil it does not follow that thinking can prevent it. But at least the habit of critical reflection puts an obstacle in the way of banal evil, for the thoughtful individual may have afterthoughts about saying or doing what he cannot account for. Moral conscience, Arendt contends, is a "side-effect" of the thinking ego, of the self who would, like Socrates, prefer that "the multitudes disagree with me than that I, being one, should be out of harmony with and contradict myself."[4]

If Heidegger simply equated moral conscience with the internalization of public expectations and sanctions, then it would be obvious why he takes the commonsense, moral interpretations of guilt and conscience to be "inauthentically oriented." But it is clear that he is *not* only criticizing the superficial form of moral conscience represented by the conformist; he argues that moral conscience as such, even in its more sophisticated, reflective, autonomous, and "postconventional" forms, and as it has been interpreted by material and formal ethics alike, "springs from the limitations of the way Dasein interprets itself in falling." He recognizes that the autonomous individual may be required to act abnormally, to behave differently than the average person would in similar circumstances because he subjects social conventions to critical appraisal in light of higher moral standards. One thinks of Martin Luther King, for example, who used to say that the call of his moral conscience gave him the strength to struggle against racial segregation even while the majority of southern Americans vehemently opposed him. Even when the morally conscientious individual happens to conform with what others demand of him he does not do so because of what they say and do but from an independent judgment as to what he ought and ought not to do. Why doesn't the presence of genuine moral conscience, then, attest to authentic individuation and freedom? On what grounds does Heidegger argue that even the morally good individual is, from a fundamental ontological standpoint, "essentially conscienceless"?

The heart of the issue is not whether one is reflective or unreflective, or whether one's stance is popular or unpopular, but whether the phenomenon of moral conscience opens one up to existence *as a whole.* And here Heidegger's answer is unequivocally negative. Even the person who embodies *Moralität* and not just *Sittlichkeit*, who puts social convention on trial before the tribunal of critical reason, is under the sway of "the Anyone,": and so no-one-in-particular. Moral conscience, on Heidegger's interpretation, "takes Dasein as something ready-to-hand to be concerned with—that is, something that gets managed and reckoned up" (*SZ*, 289). Everyday guilt stems from the failure to satisfy a moral requirement: from doing what one believes one ought not to do—an act of commission—or not doing what one believes one ought to do—an act of omission. Heidegger describes the indebtedness which one feels toward the other who has been harmed by one's deeds as involving "the not being present-at-hand of something which ought to be" (*SZ*, 283). The agent is responsible and blameworthy for a lack he has caused in the other and so he owes the victim some kind of compensation. Moral guilt is not a basic way of being of the moral agent but a factual occurrence or moral predicate. It stems from an act of transgression and is not a condition of one's finitude. One incurs a moral debt and one may pay it off. Moral conscience alerts one to one's guilt. It may warn one not to do wrong or reprove one for having done wrong. Or it may applaud one for having kept clean and maintained one's innocence. The work of moral conscience is to "concernfully reckon up 'guilt' and 'innocence' and balance them off" (*SZ*, 292).

The conscientious person, on Heidegger's reading, is a moral accountant who treats life as a business, forever worrying about whether he has covered the moral costs. He treats himself from the standpoint of a dispassionate judge or as something with which he should concern himself "as if Being-in-the-world were a household whose debts need to be balanced off so that so that the Self may stand 'by' as a disinterested spectator while these experiences run their course" (*SZ*, 293). He expects conscience to tell him specifically what it is right to do on principle and so "to provide something currently useful about assured possibilities of taking action" (*SZ*, 294). Heidegger considers moral conscience to be a way of "making certain" that he lives up to his ideals and so to reassure himself that his life is on the right track by his satisfying "manipulable rules and public norms": shared values or principles in light of which he can justify his behavior to others. It is worth noting that the German term for conscience (*das Gewissen*) derives from the root (*Wissen*) meaning certain knowledge. In abiding by the demands of moral conscience the person can account for himself by appealing to what ought to be recognized as fitting and acceptable by everyone.

That moral guilt and conscience are experiences of "the Anyone" does not entail that they are undergone by one who has forsaken his individuality by having lost himself in "the Others." Within the inauthentic domain of average everydayness Heidegger includes both the conformist who hides in the anonymity of the crowd and the autonomous moral agent who criticizes public opinion and may stand alone in the name of a higher ideal of righteousness or community. Though the moral agent does not necessarily act as "the average person" *would* in his circumstances, he does act as he believes "anyone" *should.* The "I ought to . . ." reveals the self as subject to requirements incumbent on *anyone "in my shoes"*: as bound by laws, norms, or values that claim him as one-like-others and so as essentially interchangeable for any rational or responsible agent. The measure of his action is "the universal": whether this is understood as actualizing material values or satisfying formal norms.

Heidegger does not clearly distinguish between two very different kinds of inauthenticity: (1) the *anonymity* of the unreflective person who loses himself in the crowd, and (2) the *impersonality* of the morally reflective individual who acts in light of a purportedly higher and universal standard, the supposed presence of objective values or the operation of a rational decision-procedure. What binds anonymity and impersonality as modes of inauthenticity is that they both involve a turning away from one's having to choose one's own possibilities and a turning toward possibilities that "have already been decided-upon."

Like Kierkegaard, Heidegger takes Kantian autonomy to be the paradigm of moral agency. And as Kierkegaard questions the supremacy of "the ethical" stage of existence, so Heidegger deems Kantian autonomy to be inauthentic insofar as the moral agent (1) thinks of conscience as a court of justice or the voice of reason which pronounces specific judgments in light of a universal moral law, as "the dispassionate recognition of something one can come across Objectively" (SZ, 278); (2) expects the call of conscience to disclose something positive or negative with which he can concern himself; (3) listens to conscience for determinate requirements or content, "to tell him something useful about assured possibilities of 'taking action' which are available and calculable"; and (4) makes certain that his account is balanced by reckoning up his assets and liabilities and paying off his moral debts. In the deliberation of the moral agent nothing is to be relevant except considerations that involve the situation as it would appear to anyone regardless of his past character or his psychological and historical situation, the practices that frame it and the loyalties which define his belonging to it. This model of conscientious reflection has the agent detached from his personal standpoint—from motives derived from his interests, attachments and commitments—and has him evaluating his particular will from the standpoint of impartial principles applicable to all rational agents.

What is inauthentic about the everyday, moralizing interpretation of guilt and conscience is that the orientation to specific practical injunctions stems from worldly preoccupations that close off the person to the issue of his existence as such. "We fail to recognize the disclosive character of the conscience if the tendency of the call is restricted to the indebtednesses which have already occurred or which we have before us" (SZ, 300). When guilt and conscience are understood in terms of moral indebtedness, a more fundamental demand on the self remains concealed.

The *primordial call of conscience* is uncanny because it utters no practical injunctions: it simply demands that a person face his life as a whole and suspend his tendency to secure himself by his immersion in particular projects, including moral ones. Rather than exercising the critical functions of warning, reproving, and commending by reference to claims valid for everyone, conscience in its primordial sense calls the person to the task of leading his own life without recourse to a fixed or common yardstick. Relative to the everyday expectation that conscience will provide specific "do's" and "don'ts," the existential call of conscience remains mostly unheard because it is "nothing." But a "positive content" in this "nothing" is missed when it is assumed that if the call is anything it must furnish a determinate message.

> When the call is rightly understood, it gives us that which in the existential sense is "most positive" of all—namely, the ownmost possibility which Dasein can present to itself, as a calling-back which calls it forth into its factical potentiality-for-Being-its-Self at the time. . . . Understanding the call discloses one's Dasein in the uncanniness of its individualization. . . . Wanting-to-have-a-conscience becomes a readiness-for-Anxiety. (SZ, 341–42)

The only thing I "know" in listening to the "silent call of conscience" is that I bear responsibility for what I make of the circumstances in which I find myself. The imperatives of moral conscience tempt me to be inauthentic because they promise to settle the issue of who I am to be by an appeal to a given and impersonal measure. Conscience in the primordial and "true" sense demands that a person own up to his existence as a totality. This requires acknowledging a kind of guilt that does not stem from something he did or failed to do but is the very condition of his existence.

Primordial guilt does not refer to moral transgression but to finitude. It does not mean that Dasein is lacking in something, but that "it is, in its existing, the basis of its ownmost potentiality-for-Being, although it has not laid this basis itself" (*SZ*, 284). A person is thrown into the world, subjected to it and to death, and yet remains a free being who is author of his acts and responsible for leading his own life. A person can never get a hold of his Being from the ground up, yet he is responsible for taking hold of the possibilities granted to him by his unmasterable facticity. He does not create his place, but he does shape it. Unlike things, he is involved in the constitution of his own Being. Being-guilty means that one's freedom is subject to limitations, that one's transcendence is finite, but that one remains responsible for appropriating these limiting conditions and making them one's own. In the call of conscience a person's own guilt calls him out of his absorption in the accepted and expected back to himself to acknowledge the groundlessness of his existence. Understanding the call means resolving to accept the anxiety which accompanies facing the uncertainty of Being-in-the-world. "Understanding the call is more authentic the more non-relationally Dasein hears and understands its own Being-appealed-to, and the less the meaning of the call gets perverted by what one says or by what is fitting and accepted" (*SZ*, 269). The resolute individual, in accepting the silence of the call of conscience, has surrendered all claims to a ground on which he can base his life and which would promise a final security. He does not "float above" his concrete historical situation. He is delivered over to it, but in such a way that he is called to reappropriate for himself the place to which he has already been appropriated. Being-in-the-world is *finite transcendence* or *thrown project*.

Heidegger wants to make room for our capacity to reflect on received values and norms but he attacks the "Platonic" idea that reflection involves an appeal to higher standards that would exist as entities independent of our attachments, involvements, and dispositions. In a manner consistent with Heidegger's own criticism of moral theories, Michael Walzer describes the kind of self-detachment involved in the traditional philosophical model of critical self-reflection.

> Self-criticism for the philosopher is a kind of reflection in tranquillity, a scrutiny of the self *sub specie aeternitatis*. I step back, detach myself from my self, create a new moral agent, let's call him superagent, who looks at the old one, me, as if I were a total stranger. Superagent studies me as one among others, no different from the others, and applies to all of "them," including me, objective and universal principles. Naturally, I am found wanting, but superagent is not found wanting: who could make that finding? Or, better, on what basis could such a finding be made? The psychoanalyst can criticize the superego because the superego embodies, if that is the right word, a merely particular morality. But superagent, the critical "I" imagined by the philosopher, speaks for morality itself. He is, so to speak, the philosopher's alter ego, projected into everyman.[5]

Against this traditional picture, Heidegger's model of self-reflection derives from Wilhelm Dilthey's notion of *Besinnung*: one's capacity to author one's own "Self" from the materials one is given by a critical repetition of where one already is in light of one's life as a whole.[6] This reflection does not require the radical detachment of an Ego from the world in which it is mired, or recourse to a given or fixed measure independent of time and place; the claim that such detachment is humanly possible is the fiction of metaphysics. In *Besinnung* one thinks one's life through to the end: not in order to contemplate fixed ends or goals but to find one's deepest aspirations given the preciousness of time. I am responsible for myself not because I am disengaged and detached from everyone else but because neither I nor anyone to whom I might turn for advice possesses a disinterested "view from nowhere" or god's-eye perspective on my life. I have no alternative but to choose myself from the contingent basis of my time and place.

We are now in a position to understand Heidegger's initially startling remark that being good is "essentially conscienceless" (*SZ*, 288) and that what we ordinarily call conscience is "not a conscience-phenomenon at all" (*SZ*, 292). Heidegger's defense of this view rests upon three claims about the relation between our ordinary, moral interpretation of conscience and the more primordial, existential interpretation: that, relative to the existential, the moral is (1) *partial* because it does not disclose existence as a whole, (2) *evasive* because it is motivated by a flight from anxiety, and (3) *derivative* because the capacity for moral obligation presupposes that one is guilty in one's very Being.

First, whereas moral conscience only provides *partial* access to Dasein as something "ready-to-hand" within the world whose credits and debts can be "reckoned up," existential conscience opens up Dasein's existence as a whole: as Being-unto-death ultimately grounded in nothing beyond the horizon of care or temporality itself. Dasein is not something in the world that can be handled by the calculations of a moral accountant but is most fundamentally one who must take responsibility for his own Being without recourse to a fixed measure. Dasein faces himself when he accepts that it is up to him to establish his own priorities in life: that there is no blueprint for how one ought to lead one's life as a whole.

Second, the appeal to moral conscience as a guide for one's life is a flight from or *evasion* of what the silent call of existential conscience bespeaks: the uncanniness or not-at-homeness of one's existence in its uniqueness or individuality. It takes courage to stay attuned to the anxiety that attends facing oneself alone. One is tempted to flee this mood by turning to the specific and impersonal dictates of moral conscience. The pull of moral duty tempts one, as much as the push of immediate desire, to evade the task of becoming "I-myself." Heidegger claims that the person who makes certain that he keeps a clear moral conscience is engaged in a "tranquilizing suppression of wanting-to-have-a-conscience" in the primordial, existential sense because he is not ready for the anxiety he must face if he is to hear his own voice and cease listening to the public "Anyone." Morality derives from the impersonal domain of "the Anyone" insofar as the moral "ought" announces itself as "an already-decided-upon possibility" for one who has forsaken his responsibility to explicitly choose his own possibilities. The existential conscience that calls me to anxiety in the face of my "freedom-towards-death" requires that I be "primarily unsupported by concernful solicitude."

Third, moral conscience is *derivative* of its primordial, existential counterpart. Liability to the claims of others presupposes that one is liable to existential guilt and conscience.

> That Dasein *is* guilty in the very basis of its Being is what provides, above all, the ontological condition for its ability to come to owe anything in factically existing. This essential Being-guilty is, equiprimordially, the existential condition for the possibility of the "morally" good and for that of the "morally" evil—that is, for morality in general and for the possible forms which this may take factically. The primordial "being-guilty" cannot be defined by morality, since morality already presupposes it for itself. (SZ, 286)

Only one who is guilty in his Being and is able to take responsibility for his life can incur moral obligations. The point here is not that only an authentic individual can be moral, but rather that one must be capable of authenticity, able to choose one's own existence, in order to be morally accountable to others. But if fundamental ontology shows how it is possible for Dasein to be subject to moral phenomena, this does not mean, so Heidegger insists, that a specific "ought" follows from the "is" of existence. Ontology merely lays down the conditions for morality "in all its possible factical forms." Ontology does not function as the court of jurisdiction for assessing moral theories or judgments according to whether they are appropriate to human existence.

III

The ambiguity of Heidegger's critique of morality becomes evident when we raise the following question: what is the place of moral conscience within the life of the authentic individual who honestly faces the absence of a ground that would secure and provide a measure for his existence? Although the account of the self in fundamental ontology allegedly founds the possibility of morality, it also seems to render any appeal to absolute values or norms illegitimate.

On the one hand, the warnings, reprovals and compliments of

moral conscience are not illusions to be genealogically unmasked, according to Heidegger, but are accepted as being "within their rights" (*SZ*, 279). Authenticity is not an overcoming of inauthenticity but a "modification" of it. That the voice of moral conscience is a phenomenon of inauthenticity does not mean that the authentic individual must remain unresponsive to its call, only that he must appropriate his obligations in his own way. That moral conscience does not provide authentic access to the structure of Dasein's existence as a whole does not entail that acting in a morally responsible way is "bad": so long as one does not mistake moral obligations for a more basic self-responsibility.

On the other hand, the relation between one's existential self-responsibility and moral responsibilities to others remains unclear, especially because authentic freedom-unto-death individualizes Dasein and calls into question the universal, impersonal perspective from which the self as a moral agent understands himself as just "one among others." Insofar as the individual's resolve is without foundation, the grounds for action ultimately rest upon a first-personal decision. If the task of practical philosophy is to articulate the possibility of an objective basis for preferring some alternatives over others, fundamental ontology appears to undermine such a foundationalist enterprise.

By comparing fundamental ontology to Kant's metaphysics of morals, the issue can be put in the following way. From Heidegger's point of view a metaphysics of morals is "inauthentically oriented" because it misses the "ontological essence" of the person as an end-in-itself: that a person is fundamentally self-determining not on account of his moral freedom but in virtue of his freedom-unto-death. One's most basic liability is not to the moral law but to the guilt constitutive of one's Being-in-the-world. That the self is "for its own sake" does not announce itself in the face of the moral law but in one's encounter with "the Nothing" at the ground of one's existence as a whole. "The silent call of conscience" claims one not as a moral agent capable of good and evil but as an existing individual capable of authenticity or inauthenticity, of either explicitly choosing oneself or losing oneself in already decided upon possibilities. A metaphysics of morals that takes its cue from our capacity to feel respect for the moral law, and so to be moved by ends we give to ourselves as universal subjects, screens out altogether the mood of anxiety that grants the existing individual the opportunity to choose himself without recourse to an absolute ground.

Given that the key to respect for the moral law is respect for all persons as ends-in-themselves, the question to be addressed in the following chapters is whether the obligation to give others their due announces itself from *within* the disclosure of the individual as an end-in-itself on Heidegger's terms. Does anything like Kant's kingdom of ends emerge as an ideal correlative with the "factical ideal" of authenticity? The prima facie evidence counts against this suggestion, for what distinguishes the person who faces his freedom-unto-death is that he opens himself to his own possibilities "unsupported by concernful solicitude" (*SZ*, 266). Insofar as Dasein is absorbed in its Being-with-Others it is "not I-myself." Heidegger calls the subjection of the individual to any a priori moral principle "an illusion of 'the Anyone,'" for "I-myself" am revealed in groundless resolve, not in the "self-subjecting self-elevation" of acting in accordance with duty.[7]

Once Heidegger diagnoses the feeling of respect at the heart of moral conscience as a flight from the more unsettling and fundamental mood of anxiety, morality loses its central place in the ontology of human existence, for it represents the solitary individual's escape into what Kierkegaard, referring to the ethical stage of life, calls "the security of the universal."[8] Heidegger's revision of Kant's ontological definition of the person as an end-in-himself would appear to subvert precisely what Kant's whole project was meant to defend: the centrality of moral responsibility in human life. If the authentic individual remains liable to others, it would seem that there must be a way of accounting for moral responsibility as a limiting condition on one's freedom-unto-death.

To address this concern we must turn directly to Heidegger's account of *authentic Being-towards-death.* Does the authentic individual stand in a "teleological suspension of the ethical" or "beyond good and evil"? Or does a primordial mode of moral conscience—a new capacity for responsibility to others—open up along with an authentic self-relation and give rise to a Heideggerian version of Kant's kingdom of ends? Though Heidegger claims that fundamental ontology provides the ontological foundation for any possible morality, his attack on the project of a metaphysics of morals for being guided by a reifying ontology of presence-at-hand and his insistence that Being-in-the-world as a whole is without a foundation provokes the worry that fundamental ontology erodes our moral self-understanding after all by exposing the groundlessness of all shared norms and the illusory character of all absolute claims concerning right and wrong.

There are several possibilities we must explore. The first is that fundamental ontology lays the foundation for any possible morality and any other human discipline as well but has no substantive moral content itself. The second is that *Being and Time* challenges the legitimacy of morality by showing it to be rooted in unjustified metaphysical premises that need to be overcome. Finally, *Being and Time* might offer the elements of a moral interpretation of authenticity. But if this is so, it needs to be shown how Heidegger's "existential analytic" differs from any "metaphysics of morals."

The Existentialist Interpretation: Authentic Being-unto-Death and the Authority of the Individual

I

Heidegger finds in average everydayness a clue to the ontological structure of human existence. Like Kierkegaard, he criticizes the philosophical mainstream since Descartes for taking the *cogito* to be the essence of the *sum*. Dasein, according to Heidegger, is primarily a practical being: caught up in the workaday world with things as ready-to-hand equipment and others as partners in a network of social practices. The world is not a *cosmos* fixed once and for all, or a super-object containing all objects, or a transcendental screen or categorial scheme, but is rather a cultural milieu given to Dasein in a historical *Geworfenheit* or throw: an outer horizon with which Dasein is always already familiar and to which it is oriented in a prereflective way.

But average everydayness as the site of Dasein's usual self-interpretation provides only a "provisional" clue to the structure of a person's existence as a whole. The entirety and unity of Dasein only come into play in the face of Being-unto-death when its usual understanding of itself in terms of the familiar world and the way things have been publicly interpreted breaks down and it must confront itself alone "unsupported by concernful solicitude." In anxiety Dasein faces the certainty that its life will end but the indefiniteness as to when it will end. Dasein's life-time is an incomplete, because always prospective, whole that it is responsible for integrating without recourse to a fixed yardstick or absolute measure. But first of all and most of the time Dasein has sub-mitted itself to the received network of social practices: doing and saying what "anyone" would typically do and say in its situation.

It might seem that the morally conscientious individual breaks out of the inauthenticity of "the Anyone" by calling into question pre-vailing social conventions and opinions in light of higher standards than those approved of by "society." Though Heidegger recognizes that morality makes claims on the individual that exceed what is demanded by custom or convention, he still takes moral guilt and conscience to be phenomena of inauthenticity because, as we saw in chapter 1, they are founded, partial, and evasive modes of more primordial experiences. Whether he is conventional or postconventional, unreflective or thoughtful, the person, insofar as he is morally conscientious, "has failed to take hold of *his own* possibilities." The moral viewpoint is impersonal because it directs one to possibilities that are "already decided upon" as being valid for "anyone" in one's situation. By sticking to moral princi-ples one avoids one's primary responsibility to choose oneself without appealing to a given and universal standard. That moral guilt and con-science are phenomena of inauthenticity invites the worry that the authentic individual, like Nietzsche's *Übermensch*, stands "beyond good and evil." This worry demands that we look closely at what Heidegger means by authenticity.

The first and perhaps most common interpretation of authentic-ity—one that places great emphasis on Heidegger's account of Being-unto-death but minimizes his discussions of authentic historicality and authentic Being-with-Others—associates Heidegger with the radically voluntaristic *existentialism* of Jean-Paul Sartre. Sartre is partly responsible for this affiliation because in offering his own definition of existentialism he draws heavily on Heidegger.

> When we speak of "forlornness," a term Heidegger was fond of, we
> mean only that God does not exist and that we have to face all the con-
> sequences of this. The Existentialist is strongly opposed to a certain
> kind of secular ethics which would like to abolish God with the least
> possible expense. After 1880, some French teachers tried to set up a
> secular ethics which went something like this: God is a useless and cost-
> ly hypothesis; we are discarding it; but, meanwhile, in order for there to
> be an ethics, a society, a civilization, it is essential that certain values be

taken seriously and that they be considered as having an *a priori* existence. It must be obligatory, *a priori*, to be honest, not to lie, not to beat your wife, to have children, etc., etc. So we're going to try a little device which will make it possible to show that values exist all the same, inscribed in a heaven of ideas, though otherwise God does not even exist. In other words—and this, I believe, is the tendency of everything called "reformism" in France—nothing will be changed if God does not exist. We shall find ourselves with the same norms of honesty, progress, and humanism, and we shall have made of God an outdated hypothesis which will peacefully die off by itself.

The Existentialist, on the contrary, thinks it very distressing that God does not exist, because all possibility of finding values in a heaven of ideas disappears along with Him; there can no longer be an *a priori* Good, since there is no infinite and perfect consciousness to think it. Nowhere is it written that the Good exists, that we must be honest, that we must not lie; because the fact is we are on a plane where there are only men. Dostoievski said, "If God didn't exist, everything would be possible." That is the very starting point of Existentialism. Indeed, *everything is permissible if God does not exist*, and as a result man is forlorn, because neither within him nor without does he find anything to cling to. He can't start making excuses for himself.[1]

Sartre sees Heidegger as a fellow existentialist who unmasks the illusions of impartiality, objectivity, and truth-directedness in the assertion of moral norms, and so subverts the universally binding force that moral claims are supposed to have as claims about what "one" ought to do. Freedom does not refer to the possibility of choosing between good and evil but to one's responsibility for creating standards in the first place, since there are none to be found prior to the willful act of valuation. Sartre concludes that "the death of God" means "humanism": that human beings must confer value upon possibilities without being able to appeal to a ground prior to the act of decision. If nothing is good a priori, then nothing is absolutely or irrevocably impermissible either. To draw on Sartre's own example, when I say, "It is wrong that you beat your wife," I mean that I have decided that I disapprove of it, not that it is "really" wrong for any husband to beat his wife. But if everything is permitted, then it would be right for you to beat your wife so long as you have decided that it is. I would have no way of saying that your judgment is misguided or that mine is justified because there is nothing prior to the act of valuation that make values true or false. That our valuations contradict each other does not mean that one of us is wrong: only that each of us has a different subjective perspective on the matter.

The belief that anything is absolutely impermissible is, according to Sartre, an illusion based on "Bad Faith": an evasion of one's responsibility for creating one's own values. There are no universal norms on which one can ultimately ground one's freedom. In the spirit of Sartre, Richard Rorty writes:

> Suppose that Socrates was wrong, that we have not once seen the Truth, and so will not, intuitively, recognize it when we see it again. This means that when the secret police come, when the torturers violate the innocent, there is nothing to be said to them of the form "There is something within you which you are betraying. Though you embody the practices of a totalitarian society which will endure forever, there is something beyond those practices which condemns you." This thought is hard to live with as is Sartre's remark:
>
>> Tomorrow, after my death, certain people may decide to establish fascism, and others may be miserable enough to let them get away with it. At that moment, fascism will be the truth of man, and so much the worse for us. In reality, things will be as much as man has decided they are.
>
> This hard saying brings out what ties Dewey and Foucault, James and Nietzsche [and Heidegger], together—the sense that there is nothing deep down inside us except what we have put there ourselves, no criterion that we have not created in the course of creating a practice, no standard of rationality that is not an appeal to such a criterion, no rigorous argumentation that is not obedience to our own conventions.[2]

That things do not usually seem so groundless should not fool us. Everyday life is reassuring because values seem to emanate from the world in which one is passionately engaged. But this is an illusion created by "the spirit of seriousness." When one owns up to the fact that values are the creations of human subjects, one sees that "everything is possible" and so, Sartre thinks, "all is permitted." In "the spirit of play" one affirms that values are not real but ideal and that their authority derives from the will that constitutes them. One must honestly face the fact that values are slippery: that one always already transcends one's commitments the moment one asserts them. Once a subject ceases to invest his will in a set of values, they no longer have reality for him. If they are to continue to have validity for him, he must reinvest them with meaning, knowing all the while that the moment he commits himself he is again beyond that commitment. The belief that some things are absolutely impermissible for all subjects at all times and in all places assumes that values are part of "the furniture of reality" to be discovered. This denial that we are responsible for making values is, according to Sartre, self-deception: an act of bad faith.

The famous example on which Sartre draws to illustrate that "if God is dead, then all is permitted" is the dilemma of the student who must choose whether to leave France for England to join the French Free Forces or to remain home in Paris with his dying mother who has already lost a son in the German offensive of 1940.[3] The conflict between the broad moral demands of a vast group and one's personal obligation to a single individual cannot be resolved by recourse to an impersonal decision-procedure or a priori set of norms. Who is to say whether the choice of the young man should accord with Christian, Kantian, utilitarian, or some other set of principles? Even if he adopts a particular principle to guide his choice, his choice of this rule as the appropriate one to guide him would already be determined by his subjective outlook. And it is by no means clear that any general rule will tell him the right course of action to adopt. This is because no one course is *the* right one. It is up to him to decide for himself which alternative he can best live with.

Sartre identifies the subject's judgment that a particular end is good with the "leap of faith" by which Abraham decides that the mandate to kill his son, Isaac, is the voice of an angel appointed by God. One cannot avoid the subjective element in decision and so the anguish of first-personal responsibility for how to approach one's situation. The military leader who must either send his men to death for the greater good or else protect his soldiers but thereby jeopardize the cause for which they are fighting knows what it means to face a situation without the comfort of a fixed measure that would validate what is best.

But the lesson that Sartre draws from his examples—that evaluation is ultimately a wholly subjective act of commitment—misrepresents the judgments that the heroes of these examples make. That no one course of action is *the* right one does not preclude that some alternatives may be clearly wrong; these would be morally irresponsible choices even if one took responsibility for them, and partly because one was capable of doing so. The situations of the student and the general are both compelling because the alternatives that each of them faces have good reasons or morally relevant considerations to support them. The structure of their dilemmas is not like Abraham's since his is a choice between a moral and a grossly immoral (though possibly religious) alternative, not between two morally attractive possibilities. In cases of moral dilemmas like those of the student and the general, there may be no impersonal, much less human-independent, criterion telling one which way to go; but the range of morally acceptable possibilities is not arbitrarily determined by the will of an individual subject.

Suppose that the young man felt torn between the possibilities of either staying with his sick mother or collaborating with the Nazis out of sympathy for their cause and a desire to get ahead in the new social order under the Vichy government. Though the fact that this feels like a dilemma to him betrays his subjective outlook—an outlook that allows the alternative of collaboration to seem not only attractive but even morally required of him—his subjective experience does not give each possibility *legitimate* moral weight. What is illegitimate about collaboration is that it is in fact wrong even if it seems right to him. To see that this is so does require that we be human subjects capable of recognizing the difference between right and wrong. But this does not mean that the individual invents his standards or that he is accountable only in terms of the norms that seem compelling from his perspective. Likewise, the dilemma for a general who must choose between telling the truth about a disastrous venture he commanded and lying in order to protect his reputation is understandable as a conflict between the hard road of doing what is right and the temptation to choose what is expedient; but it is not a moral dilemma and his decision to cover up does not erase the moral requirement of forthrightness. Indeed it is precisely the presence of this requirement in the face of his violating it that constitutes his blameworthiness.

Charles Taylor properly contends that we cannot understand the nature of our self-responsibility on Sartre's model of "radical choosing."[4] Sartre is correct that persons are self-responsible agents because they are not simply driven by first-order desires and motives but choose to be moved by certain desires and motives in light of their evaluations. One's values, the kind of person one really wants to be, are not simply the product of first-order desires or the outcome of a process of calculation or "simple weighing" which aims at maximum overall satisfaction by balancing off short- and long-term desires. "Simple weighing" is a form of what Taylor calls "weak evaluation." Rather, a person is a "strong evaluator" who characterizes his desires not quantitatively but qualitatively: in terms of the kind of person he aspires to be. He may refrain from letting certain desires and motives affect his will not because these first-order impulses are outweighed by other desires but because he judges these motives to be *unworthy* of him.

Human motivation has "depth" because "our desires do not motivate only by virtue of the attraction of their consummations";[5] we characterize desires "contrastively" in terms of the quality of life they express. For the "simple weigher" all desires represent goods; the only issue is whether their satisfaction would be in one's long-range best interests. For the "strong evaluator," on the other hand, one's desires may not be goods even in themselves for their satisfaction may violate one's higher aspirations. Strong evaluation is an essential characteristic of self-responsibility; a weak evaluator has no executive "Self" because he is just the vehicle of desires that push him one way or another. A strong evaluator is responsible in three respects. First, he is responsible for what he does because he chooses to be moved by first-order desires and motives in light of his values. Second, he is responsible for the degree to which he acts in line with his evaluations; that he is capable of acting in accordance with his ideals does not entail that he does so. Third, he is responsible for these values or ideals themselves; it is up to him to decide what is worthy of him.

But what is it to be responsible for one's own evaluations? Sartre's view is that authenticity or lucid self-responsibility requires facing up to the anguishing fact that values rest ultimately on the act of espousing them, not on reasons. Taylor, however, claims that construing self-responsibility as being a matter of "radical choosing" generates a paradox. Sartre insists on the importance of our remaining lucidly aware of our freedom, possibilities, and choices. But for freedom to amount to choice requires that alternatives appear in terms of their relative *desirability*; otherwise, choice is capricious and there seems to be no good reason to be aware of one's freedom. Being authentic is important if it allows us to appreciate the most desirable alternatives; for if it only lets us see that no one possibility is really more desirable than any others, why prefer lucidity to bad faith?

Sartre's examples give his conception of self-responsibility as radical choosing "a semblance of plausibility" because by focusing on moral dilemmas he overlooks the point that the basis of such dilemmas lies not in radical choice but in the *revealed importance* of rival moral claims or obligations each of which is already given as being a desirable alternative.[6] A moral dilemma is a radical choice *between* strong evaluations, but not a radical choice *of* such evaluations in the first place. The example of the young man faced with the alternatives of joining the French Resistance or tending to his sick mother is a moral dilemma because the young man is confronted with two powerful moral claims or obligations, not just possibilities he happens to have invested with value. His options are experienced as obligations before he gives them weight in a self-conscious act of will. That this is a moral dilemma means that the young man cannot dissolve the predicament by simply declaring one of the claims "dead and inoperative." The determination of his obligations does not issue from radical choice even if his choice between them is ultimately "subjective." But the priority of arbitrary resolve in Sartre's idea of authentic freedom leaves no room for judgments like "I *owe* it to my mother" or "I *have* a responsibility to my countrymen"; for the importance of these possibilities is given in an evaluation "constated," not chosen, and revealed as a prior claim or obligation upon the freedom of the responsible subject.

That I am free not to live up to a moral requirement does not imply that I create its obligatory force in the first place. That the authority of a moral requirement depends on my relationship to it does not mean that I constitute it; rather, I find myself subject to the demand it makes on my will. It is true that I am fully governed by a moral requirement insofar as I am able to see its "point" for myself and not because others happen to demand it of me. Cruel, dishonest, and selfish acts are prima facie wrong and ought to be avoided not because I might be punished for them but because in them I do harm to others "for no good reason." This is why punishment would be justified. That the obligation to be relatively kind, honest, and fair is a nuisance to a vicious person does not mean that he is exempt from the obligations to avoid cruelty, dishonesty, and selfishness. We assume that he—unlike animals and young children—"knows better." What he ought to will does not necessarily conform to what he in fact wills. In this regard basic moral requirements exist independent of and prior to his personal act of valuation.

This does not mean that moral obligations exist independent of human subjects altogether as if there is some "heaven" of moral "values." The presence in the world of what ought to be relates to the possible experience of a morally responsible subject. That an obligation is independent of the will of a particular individual does not mean that it has its source beyond human beings, but only that it is a morally relevant consideration for the agent even if he does not honor it. The prima facie wrongness of collaboration with the Nazis has force independent of the young man's will because it provides a good reason for choosing to resist whether he is committed to the resistance or not. The abilities to recognize the evil of the Nazi occupation and to articulate what is unjust about it does presuppose that the young man has sufficient moral character to appreciate what is morally relevant in his situation. But having the character to acknowledge moral truisms is not a choice he makes; it is more like a station he finds himself occupying given that he has received a good upbringing and has the right sort of basic responses.

Sartre's examples do not show us what he thinks they do: that because no decision is absolutely justified or right in these cases, therefore "everything is permitted" and no alternatives would be unjustified. It simply does not follow from the claim that human subjectivity is the *condition* of there being moral values that the free subject is the *source* of all values. That the difference between right and wrong, or good and evil, depends on the existence of human agents subject to praise and blame does not imply that individuals invent moral "values" on the basis of nothing. And it does not follow from the claim that everything is *possible* that everything is *permissible*. Even if the subject is always free in that no motive or reason *compels* him to choose one alternative over others, this does not entail that "nothing, absolutely nothing, *justifies* me in adopting this or that particular value, this or that particular scale of values." If I am condemned not just to be free but to be morally free, then I am just as condemned to moral responsibility as I am to self-responsibility.

It is true, of course, that no consideration or argument or principle can compel me to *own up* to my moral responsibilities to others. It is for me to decide whether to do the morally responsible or irresponsible thing—but I do not decide whether to *be* morally responsible. Liability for the harm I do to others is a defining aspect of my humanity. And it is true that even if I decide to honor my moral obligations to others, there is no single way of determining just what the worthiest course of action would be in a particular situation. I must judge just how to exercise my capacity for moral responsibility. It is also the case that the range of my moral obligations depends in part on the particular projects I have undertaken. And it is true finally that the range of what is morally obligatory vastly underdetermines the choices I make in life. But none of these indeterminacies implies that no possibilities are absolutely impermissible, morally speaking: that because I would be equally justified choosing any of a number of possibilities I would be equally justified doing anything and so would not be absolutely unjustified doing anything.

II

If it is fair to equate Heidegger's "factical ideal" of authentic freedom-unto-death with Sartre's notion of lucid freedom, then Heidegger is liable to the same criticism that convicts Sartre: that the sense in which individuals are responsible for themselves cannot be captured on the existentialist model of the self as a "radical chooser." One thinker who clearly interprets Heidegger's image of authentic existence as voluntaristic and existentialist is Frederic Olafson. He writes that Heidegger's ontology eliminates value-qualities from Being and replaces older concepts of ethical knowledge or truth with the idea of an *Entwurf* or project. There is no validation of our projects by reference to preexisting rules, truths, or values of any kind.

> Both Heidegger and Sartre emphatically deny that human beings can properly be said to *know* what is morally required of them in a way that is genuinely independent of their own individual choices. . . . They repudiate in principle the use of the concepts of truth and falsity in moral contexts. . . . The choices we think of ourselves as making on the basis of certain morally relevant features of a situation are only the visible tip of a much more radical choice which includes that analysis itself. It also means that no feature of any state of affairs can confer on itself the status of being what is called a "good-making consideration" or reason, and that it acquires this status only within the context of the very system of evaluative preferences for which it is supposed to provide some measure of independent support. The force of the existentialist thesis that to treat some feature of an existing situation as a reason is—implicitly at least—to choose or decide that it should be one, is to remind us that once we understand the underivability of our evaluative judgments from anything that could be called a truth (whether necessary or contingent), we have no alternative but to espouse them as our own choices.[7]

Though in themselves things just are, we transcend them in pursuit of our goals and so invest them with meaning. Human beings necessarily understand their situation in terms of some future outcome to which they have committed themselves and which they seek to bring about by their own efforts. To face our situation honestly requires accepting the absence of any framework of principles within which choice could assume its Aristotelian sense of deliberation about means to predefined ends. All questions about which possible course of action is to be chosen remain open and can be resolved for each person only by that person's actual decision for which he bears a unique responsibility.

Olafson admits that an existentialist ethic recognizes at least one positive virtue: authenticity or the capacity for living in full awareness and acceptance of one's ontological situation and the radical freedom it entails. Persons usually seek to suppress such self-knowledge by immersing themselves in the public and collective medium: *das Man* or "the Anyone." But in public life the first-personal character of existence and action is blurred by an illusory sense of there being determinate, preestablished norms. If ontological courage or resoluteness is the sole existential virtue, then how can Heidegger avoid a nihilistic doctrine of action for action's sake? Fundamental ontology appears to offer no basis for any shared moral standards except those that are arrived at inauthentically and so trace to a flight from the solitude of first-personal decision into "the security of the universal." Olafson concludes that Heidegger "makes no contribution to the moral relations in which human beings stand to one another."[8] And beyond that we have seen in Taylor's criticism of Sartre that one has no good reason to strive for authenticity, for a lucid awareness of one's own freedom, if this does not help one to recognize the relative desirability of alternative courses of action.

Heidegger surely invites this existentialist interpretation and so makes himself vulnerable to the charges that his philosophy is radically individualistic, egocentric, voluntaristic, and decisionistic. The problem with Heidegger's account of authenticity is that the nonrelational, individualizing character of Being-towards-death appears to subvert the prior claim that others have on my will insofar as I am a moral agent. The centrality and tone of the death-analysis makes it seem like the experience of my mortality, rather than revealing me not to be the center of the world, shows just the opposite: that the significance of entities within my world depends wholly on my projects. The individuating power of Being-towards-death drives a wedge between the self and nature and between the individual and the community. Heidegger's insistence that anxiety and authenticity do not take us out of the world but lead to a more primordial engagement does not resolve the tensions between Being-unto-death on the one hand and Being-in-the-world and Being-with-Others on the other.

Because there is no ontological room at the level of authenticity for the experience of obligation, morality appears as just one among many inauthentic possibilities I may or may not appropriate. The only imperatives binding on me are those that I invest with authority on the basis of groundless resolve. If there is no higher law than that of "the Anyone," then it would appear that the authentic individual stands outside the law or "beyond good and evil." Hans Jonas compares Heidegger's authentic individual to the gnostic ideal of the *pneumaticos* or spiritual man.

> Heidegger rejects any definable "nature" which would subject his sovereign existence to a predetermined essence and thus make him part

of an objective order of essences in the totality of nature. In this conception of a transessential, freely "self-projecting" existence I see something comparable to the gnostic concept of the transpsychical negativi-
ty of the *pneuma.* That which has no nature has no norm. Only that
which belongs to an order of natures—be it an order of creation, or of
intelligible forms—can have a nature. Only where there is a whole is
there a law. In the deprecating view of the Gnostics this holds for the
psyche, which belongs to the cosmic whole. Psychical man can do no better than abide by a code of law and strive to be just, that is, properly
"adjusted" to the established order, and thus play his allotted part in
the cosmic scheme. But the *pneumaticos,* "spiritual" man, who does not
belong to any objective scheme, is above the law, beyond good and evil,
and a law unto himself in the power of his "knowledge."[9]

For Heidegger, as for Kierkegaard, the particular is higher than the universal. But without recourse to the religious the particular is not grounded in a law higher and more severe than the universal. The implication
would seem to be that the authentic individual is an antinomian self
beholden only to claims issuing from his own, arbitrary self-assertion.
The silence of Abraham's personal relationship with God is replaced by
"the silent call of conscience." But now one's secrecy—one's being
beyond justifications demanded by the universal—is not grounded in a
relation to the transcendent but in one's relation to oneself alone.

Even if it is an incomplete portrait, Heidegger is responsible for
conveying the impression that the authentic individual is a "solitary hero
pitted over against an anonymous, inauthentic public as an iconoclastic
rebel rejecting the conformist mass: a figure who is all erratic originality
repudiating the humdrum conformity of average everydayness and
asserting his own 'authority.'"[10] On the existentialist reading, "facticity"
means an inert "in itself" upon which meaning must be cast arbitrarily,
and "resolve" implies the acceptance of a vertiginous freedom requiring
a detachment of the individual from all his prior connections and dispositions.

Heidegger seems to situate Dasein so that it must posit values on
the basis of nothing—without warrant from any theological or cosmo-
logical background-order or human essence we are meant to realize.
Even if meaning is first of all and most of the time a collective, not an
individual, project, *Being and Time* is haunted, as Joseph Fell points out,
by the specter of transcendental idealism.

The internal relations of the world ultimately succumb to a Nihilism
that leaves pure present-at-hand *existentia* intrinsically devoid of any

meaning as the sole mode of constancy freeing Dasein to regard meaning or *essentia* as a meta-physical creation of the decisive will. Since the
essence and value of existence are cognitively absent, they must be sup-
plied without ground by a transcendental-subjective act of faith, will or
choice exercised independent of any past.[11]

So long as meaning is projected on beings that are inherently
"absurd" (*wiedersinnig*) no reconciliation between existence and essence,
actuality and ideality, is possible (*SZ*, 151). As Stanley Rosen writes:

> If "the world is everything that is the case," or the value-free fact of all
> facts, then the facticity of those facts has itself no value. Facticity is
> merely a synonym for transcience. The significance of "what is the case"
> depends not on the fact that it is the case, but upon the peculiar fact of
> human consciousness, that is, of the (nihilistic) consciousness which
> grasps the intrinsic valuelessness of the factic. It is not the facts that
> count, but their significance; and their significance has nothing to do
> with their facticity. This is the paradoxical inference from the primacy
> of facticity: to persevere in the face of the value-free is to become free
> for the projection of value. . . . The nihilist perseveres in the face of
> despair not because he has a reason for so doing, but because his osten-
> sible comprehension of the worthlessness of all reasons is understood
> by him as freedom.[12]

Heidegger's emphasis on the unity and wholeness of Dasein leads
him to grant as much power to death and the individual as he does.
Death looms less important when one stresses that a person exists not as
a self-sufficient whole but as part of a community and a larger and elusive
reality. The desire for unity aroused by my death—the desire to confer
the stamp of authorship on my life as a whole rather than to be buffeted
about by the pressures of social life—stands in an uneasy relationship
with the desire to exist as part of a larger whole to which I belong and in
light of which I gain importance as a participant in, and contributor to,
a larger narrative. In Heidegger's stress on the individual alone and facing death outside the context of social relations, there is a tendency to
see Being-with-Others as the site where the individual loses himself by
delivering himself over to "the Anyone." Surely there is a difference,
however, between being a part of a whole by being lost in "the Anyone"
and belonging to a larger reality by being open to others as "Thou." But
if care is always care-for-self and authentic relations are only built on the
way one is grounded in oneself, it seems that there is an irreducible pri-

vacy or egocentricity built into the structures of fundamental ontology.

By granting so much authority to the isolated and detached individual, Heidegger sustains what Iris Murdoch takes to be the common failing of continental and Anglo-American philosophy—in both their rationalist and existentialist varieties—in the first half of the twentieth-century: namely, "that we have been left with far too shallow and flimsy an idea of human personality."[13] On this reading—and here we recall Olafson's identification of Heidegger and Sartre as partners in the project of radical voluntarism—the authentic individual is symptomatic of a loss of moral substance in our conception of ourselves.

> We no longer see man against a background of values, of realities, which transcend him. We picture man as a brave naked will surrounded by an easily comprehended empirical world. For the hard idea of truth we have substituted a facile idea of sincerity. What we have never had, of course, is a satisfactory Liberal theory of personality, a theory of man as free and separate *and* related to a rich and complicated world from which, as a moral being, he has much to learn. We have bought the Liberal theory as it stands, because we have wished to encourage people to think of themselves as free, at the cost of surrendering the background.[14]

It is the background that always places the person in a prior context of reasons or "good-making considerations." The problem, on Murdoch's view, is not that the individual is poised over and against a factic world that makes no claims on him prior to his giving value to it, but rather that the world in which one is involved is all too full of promptings that can only be integrated by the suppression of some or by an effort of clarification and articulation in the course of which the very nature of what one cares about may be altered.

One never stands wholly outside what Bernard Williams calls the "thick concepts"—like cruelty, lying, treachery, brutality, and gratitude—in terms of which the world is understood; and these concepts reveal the artificiality of trying to carve the world up into facts and values expressed by way of neatly divided descriptive and prescriptive discourses.[15] As Frithjof Bergmann writes:

> The world does not consist of neutral objects which we disdain or value; the world is sad and alluring, horrible, magnificent and disgusting, attractive, splendid and mean *in its own right*. . . . As long as the world is seen as a gray collage of facts one problem stands unavoidably at the

center: the question of how values are "justified." If the given is thought to be bare fact, and values are conceptualized as fundamentally different, the issue of their entrance, of their arrival in this stage domain, has to arise. From the outset, the discussion takes the form of a search: where in the great wall of facts is the chink through which values are supposed to come in? And what gives them a creditable base? This is now radically changed. There is of course still a problem of "justification": but it is longer has the same meaning, or the same size. To say it first bluntly: there no longer is any question about how values "come in," or about the nature of their "derivation" from facts, for the plain reason that they are there from the beginning, and that they are not "secondary" to the facts.[16]

When justification is an issue, it is not for a self who is isolated and detached from the world, but for one who experiences the conflicting claims and possibilities that present themselves for anyone who is sensitive to the depth of the world. A subtle appreciation of freedom requires a recovery of the background—of "the rich and complicated world from which one, as a moral being, has much to learn"—and, according to Murdoch, this calls for nothing less than an attack on the "thin" image of the self that existentialism propounds.

> We need to be enabled to think in terms of degrees of freedom, and to picture, in a non-metaphysical, non-totalitarian and non-religious sense, the transcendence of reality. A simpleminded faith in science, together with the assumption that we are all rational and totally free, engenders a dangerous lack of curiosity about the real world, a failure to appreciate the difficulties of knowing it. We need to return from the self-centered concept of sincerity to the other-centered concept of truth. We are not isolated free choosers, monarchs of all we survey, but benighted creatures sunk in a reality whose nature we are constantly tempted to deform by fantasy. Our current picture of freedom encourages a dream-like facility; whereas what we require is a renewed sense of the difficulty and complexity of the moral life and the opacity of persons. We need concepts in terms of which to picture the substance of our being; it is through an enriching and deepening of concepts that moral progress takes place. Simone Weil said that morality was a matter of attention, not of will. We need a new vocabulary of attention.[17]

III

But Heidegger rejects being labeled an "existentialist," for the idea that individuals are responsible for creating values *ex nihilo* presupposes a Cartesian dualism between subjects and objects that fundamental ontology aims to overcome. Heidegger sees himself as attacking a "humanism" that assumes a "worldless" subject projecting values upon a neutral field of objects. The structures of Being-in-the-world provide precisely the background—in Heidegger's terms, the "thrownness"—that permits us to see Dasein as a situated being always already claimed by dimensions anterior to its own projects.

Heidegger's account of "anticipation"—that we are always oriented toward the to-be, toward a possible future that transcends the limits of the past even as it is built on the past—must be rooted in his analysis of "resolve"—that we are responsible for taking hold of our situation even though we can never master our Being from the ground up. One is never absolutely free in the sense that one would be unaffected or uninfluenced by the historical setting in which one lives. The authentic individual is never untainted by inauthenticity. One is related not to abstract or fantastical possibilities—as if one were unconstrained by time and place—but to actual possiblities whose compelling character is granted by the particular historical horizon to which one inextricably belongs.

Authenticity does not put the individual in the position of being "a monarch of all he surveys," for being awakened to one's death and thrownness recalls one to the finitude in which one's projects are always embedded: to the impossibility of "surveying" one's existence from some standpoint of impartiality. One's relationship to one's life is always defined by actual and possible commitments, and these are in turn rooted in a factical situation that ever exceeds one's "grasp." Heidegger seeks to recover what Murdoch calls "the substance of our being" from rationalisms and existentialisms alike that would set a worldless ego or ideal observer over and against the world understood as a neutral, objective medium.

The fact/value, is/ought, and descriptive/prescriptive distinctions presuppose an object/subject dichotomy that Heidegger calls into question because it gives priority to a theoretical relation between self and world: a posture in which a valuing self stands essentially apart from a world of value-free facts. The substantiality—one might say the "density"—of the world means that Dasein is always in it and is exceeded by its claims even when Dasein faces itself alone in order to take hold of its own possibilities. It is possible to understand authenticity in Simone

Weil's terms not as freeing the individual from the world and leaving him an isolated will but rather as freeing one to pay attention to the world in a way that is not governed by how things have been publicly interpreted.[18]

From a stance of attentiveness one can "let beings be" so that they show themselves in ways that are missed from the perspective of everyday taken-for-grantedness. Authenticity does not deprive one of the content of the world but allows fresh access to it. But this anti-existentialist reading of authentic freedom-unto-death requires that we pay attention to Heidegger's insistence that although "anxiety individualizes Dasein and discloses it as 'solus ipse'" because in anxiety "the 'world' can offer nothing more, and neither can the Dasein-with of others," nonetheless

> Resoluteness, as authentic Being-one's-Self, does not detach Dasein
> from its world, nor does it isolate it so that it becomes a free-floating
> "I." And how should it, when resoluteness as authentic disclosedness, is
> authentically nothing else than Being-in-the-world? Resoluteness brings
> the Self right into its current concernful Being-alongside what is ready-
> to-hand, and pushes it into solicitous Being with others. (SZ, 298)

It remains to be seen whether the way in which Dasein is brought back into the world restores to its freedom the moral substance that is missing when authentic self-responsibility is conceived on the Sartrean model of "radical choosing."

From Heidegger's perspective, Sartre's existentialism is part of the modern metaphysics of subjectivity that finds the measure of Being in the human subject. Existentialism is based on the axioms of Cartesian philosophy: the transparent and self-sufficient presence of the subject to itself, the self-affection by which the subject is assured of its self-certainty, the dualism of ego and non-ego, and the positing of the human subject as the sole source of all meaning. For Heidegger, by contrast, humanity is not an origin but an answer to, or correspondence with, the "sending" of Being. Human projection is not a pure upsurging of subjectivity outside the passive in-itself, but rather a response to an always prior and encompassing thrownness. Dasein does not create, but is open to, the dimension of the possible; possibility refers to a temporal structure that is not possessed by, but possesses, Dasein.

Authenticity, far from freeing one for a radical originality, lets one appreciate the depth of the world to which one is already committed. As Joseph Fell puts it, Heidegger is trying in *Being and Time* to combat nihilism without reference to an unconditioned, permanent being as a metaphysical ground of conditioned, temporal beings.[19] If freedom is transcendence toward the Being of beings, what it calls for is not the courage of living in sheer groundlessness but the courage of owning up to a historical ground: a relative and finite ground to which Dasein always already belongs and in which it participates. As finite, this ground is groundless, for it is relative and historical and not itself grounded in the unconditioned. But it remains a ground nonetheless because it is the always prior basis of Dasein's projects: a basis over which Dasein never has power or mastery—for Dasein is thrown into it.

The recovery of a meaningful world in the face of the absence of metaphysically sanctioned meaning requires a resolute renunciation of two extreme assumptions: (1) the view that meaning must reside in the unconditioned or nowhere at all—in which case all conditioned beings are devalued; and (2) the view that meaning resides only in the individual subject who projects values on things in light of arbitrarily willed acts of commitment. As Fell puts it: "When judged by the standards of the unconditioned, world is unstable. But when judged by the standards of nihilism, world is the precedent community of meaning that nihilism has overlooked."[20] The existentialist has supposed that meaning must be either objective or subjective: if values are not given, they must be made, invented, created *ex nihilo*. This assumes that in the absence of an unconditioned, *objective* ground the *subject* is unconditioned: that it must freely project values on neutral facts. But the world one belongs to is never a neutral fact, even from the perspective of anxiety.

The real issue in owning up to one's freedom-unto-death is not rebellion or originality but appropriation: the recognition that, whatever roles and values I assume, it is I who choose them in the end, one way or another. The rebel who claims absolute originality for his projects reacts against the past and so is tied to it as much as the conformist who submissively repeats it. Appropriation does not involve creation out of nothing; the content for one's choice of self inevitably comes from the past. Meaning is always present and socially constituted; I am only through language and the social relations, practices, and institutions it enables. My facticity, situation, or past grants me a plurality of meaningful possibilities. But it is freedom or transcendence bounded by the horizon of death that lets me put what has been handed down to me in perspective for myself. Authentic resolve is not freedom from the past but through it. Even new and unforeseen possibilities do not attest to a free-floating subject but are forged from what already is. The call of conscience does not awaken me to a vertiginous freedom in the face of which I must create values without justification, but to a personal fate rooted in an inherited past bearing on the destiny of the community to which I belong.

Though death brings me before my life as my own to lead—and reminds me that it is up to me to take stock and make sense of my time and place—individuation does not mean cutting off attachments and connections. *Besinnung* is not reflective detachment, but determining what really counts in the face of the possibility of loss or non-Being as the horizon of my Being-in-the-world. Anxiety in the face of my Being-unto-death does not put me in the position of a "radical chooser" poised over against meaningless facticity. Freedom is not the experience of the absence of claims but an awakening to the issue of which claims I can call my own. The point is not to be aware that nothing matters but to recognize that how things matter to me is my responsibility: that there is no neutral metalanguage or fixed yardstick for assessing rival self-interpretations.

An authentic relation to one's Being-unto-death is not self-preoccupying so much as world-revealing. Death confers on existence "the mobile rhythm of a discursus" whose sense constitutes itself as a musical whole always on the move.[21] Simply living through the polyphony does not guarantee its coherence. The tragic wisdom provided by my mortality—that there is not time for everything, that it is not true that everything returns and that not everything can be reversed—lets me see what really matters to me, what I most deeply care about, as opposed to what I take for granted in the course of daily worries. This awareness does not awaken me to the emptiness or arbitrariness of my choices but to their gravity given the felt importance of the things that claim me when I take my time seriously. To see my life comprehensively and as mine to lead without recourse to an absolute measure is to recognize that I can waste time by staying stuck for fear of risking change. The irony here is that anxiety over choosing for oneself and risking change traces to anxiety in the face of death; and yet a life stuck in time is a kind of living death. To let death have "its rightful power over life" is to accept the ultimacy of time: to give up the will to a timeless ground, a will rooted in the need to secure oneself against the terrors of transience, chance, and finally death.

Heidegger points toward overcoming the existentialist version of nihilism by his insistence that our existence is never at our disposal. I am always caught up in a particular historical and biographical situation; there is no Archimedean standpoint outside my past and the cares of my commitments from which to survey my possibilities. We do not ground our own Being-in-the-world, yet we are responsible for reappropriating a place to which we have already been appropriated. Dasein depends on a groundless ground that is not at its disposal and is independent of its arrangements. Thrownness does not precede my projection but is already determined as pastness, as the historical site governing my possibilities. I am not a "radical chooser" floating unhinged above value-free facticity but am already involved in a heritage: a context of importance that discloses limits and possibilities. To act capriciously, without concern for my past, is not the height of, but the absence of, self-responsibility.

Those who claim that fundamental ontology is egocentric and oblivious to, if not subversive of, the moral dimension often attribute this to the centrality of the death-analysis in Heidegger's account of authenticity. Heidegger follows Kierkegaard in making anxiety the most important phenomenon of existence. Anxiety opens one to the uncanniness of existence, to finitude without refuge: to the dizziness of authentic freedom-unto-death. In anxiety, the individual seems to be preoccupied with himself and unavailable to—perhaps even incapable of meaningful relationships with—others. A key characteristic of Dasein in its authentic encounter with Being-unto-death is its "*non-relationality*": that "the potentiality-for-Being in which its ownmost Being is an issue must be taken over *alone*." The solitude of the authentic individual suggests one who stands above and beyond the world in pure transcendence: one who is in retreat from the world. Heidegger's portrayal of average everydayness— the home of one's Being-with-Others—as the site of corruption supports the sense that the price of transcendence is world-renunciation. Once the self is deprived of the content provided by its engagement in the world and with others, it is thrown back on itself as an empty ego without the resources—the desires, motives, energy—that would orient it toward the world.

Yet Heidegger insists time and again that the nonrelational individuality occasioned by authentic freedom-unto-death does not leave Dasein a worldless subject "floating above" the world or over against a neutral field of facts upon which it must project meaning arbitrarily. Conscience does not call one to retreat from the world or to renounce it, but to be in it without being of it: to open oneself to things and others without understanding oneself primarily in terms of the way the world has been interpreted publicly. The point is not to be out of this world but to be involved in it without being lost to "the others." That existence is mine, that life is first-personal, that ultimately I am responsible for what I make of my circumstances, by no means precludes my desire for love, friendship, and community or implies that I must treat others primarily as means to my own ends without any feeling of moral responsibility to them. But the question still remains: If authentic transcendence does not involve world-renunciation, just how does it alter one's Being-in-the-world and especially one's Being-with-Others?

We have seen that Heidegger is responsible for the existentialist interpretation of authenticity. The collapse of freedom into arbitrary decision is invited by his own emphasis on the nonrelational solitude of authentic Being-unto-death. But Heidegger repudiates the label "existentialist." He emphasizes that Dasein should not be thought over and against the world to which it belongs and that anticipatory resoluteness is not so self-enclosed. *Authentic Being-unto-death* exists in a vacuum unless it is understood in the context of "*authentic historicality.*" To the latter we must now turn to see whether the rooting of Dasein in its historical time and place lends to authenticity a moral substance that is missing when authenticity is interpreted primarily in terms of the death-analysis.

3

The Historicist Interpretation: Authentic Historicality and the Authority of Tradition

I

Through the lens of a reading of *Being and Time* that puts weight on Heidegger's account of Dasein's "historicality," the existentialist interpretation, which places so much emphasis on Being-unto-death, looks one-sided. The principle of historicality—the idea that authentic existence demands the subordination of the individual to a "communal destiny"—calls into question the interpretation of fundamental ontology as a radical individualism that estranges the person from his community and places him "beyond good and evil."

The existentialist interpretation mistakenly embraces as Heidegger's own the very dualism of subject-object he intends to criticize by means of his hermeneutics of the *sum*. The existentialist takes the meaningless universe projected by the objectifying reduction of the knowing-representing subject to be the world as it is "in itself." Displaced from any prior context of significance, the "free" subject is responsible for creating meaning *ex nihilo* by throwing values over a neutral field of objects. The catchphrase of existentialist individualism—that the subject makes himself because he is absolutely free to create his own values—presupposes the very metaphysics of subjectivity from which Heidegger distances himself when, in his "Letter on Humanism," he calls fundamental ontology a "fundamental ethics" and denies that he is an existentialist. Historicality is the principle intended to prevent fundamental ontology from lapsing into the kind of subjectivism of which Olafson, among others, accuses it.

What I shall call the historicist reading of *Being and Time* grants equiprimordiality to facticity and transcendence, to thrownness and projection. One can never absolutely rise above the particular time and place into which one has been cast: the heritage and community to which one already belongs and which one can never wholly master "from the ground up." The atomistic subject of existentialism is an abstraction because freedom arises as the reappropriation of a social context of meaning in which one already participates. That Being-in-the-world as a whole is a groundless ground does not make Dasein's choices arbitrary, for plausible possibilities emerge from a concrete situation in which one is caught up. History is not something over against a subject but is the lived context from out of which one's limited possibilities emerge. That history is personal does not mean that it is the product of an individual's meaning-constituting will. The individual is always already social and historical, yet free to thoughtfully respond to her heritage or to lose herself in it.

Not to have lost oneself means that one has found one's own way from within one's heritage, not that one stands outside its influence. Heidegger assures us that "resoluteness, as authentic Being-one's-Self, does not detach Dasein from its world, nor does it isolate it so that it becomes a free-floating 'I'" (*SZ*, 298). While Being-unto-death individuates Dasein it does not subjectivize him; "the Self" is not an internal, subjective being radically distinct from external, objective projects and situations. Rather than transporting Dasein from the actual world to other possible worlds where one would be a different person by engaging in other life-projects, authentic Being-unto-death leads to the appreciation of one's *finite* freedom: to a recognition of the compelling situation of the actual historical world and to an urgent commitment to what is most unique about one's way of being-there. Only as a member of a community with a shared heritage does one seek to own up to one's fate in relation to a wider destiny "we" all face.

We must explore just how Dasein's place in the community is understood within Heidegger's idea of "authentic historicality." How does the ontological character of Dasein's historicality bear on what it means to dwell authentically? How is one's personal fate tied to communal destiny and one's own finite freedom related to the freedom of others? Even if the individual is inextricably bound to the larger community, this will not be enough to show that fundamental ontology is sufficient as a "fundamental ethics," for it may only imply that the individual's possibilities are always conditioned by conventional, parochial conceptions of good and evil. This would leave unanswered the question of whether there is a measure for evaluating different local moralities or for mediating among competing conceptions of the good within a community.

Up to the discussion of historicality four-fifths of the way through *Being and Time*, nothing has been said about the *content* of Dasein's resolve. Though we know that authentic Dasein projects itself upon possibilities that are uniquely its own, this remains a wholly formal stipulation that does not exclude anything. But it is surely not the case that anything goes for a historically situated freedom. I may be able to imagine but I cannot live the world through the perspective of an ancient Athenian landowner, a medieval astrologer, or even a contemporary Sudanese nomad. My very effort to imagine how the horizon of their possibilities opens up for them is mediated by the possibilities that are real for me here and now. Though ontology has no business trying to decide "what Dasein *factically* resolves in any particular case," that does not rule out its asking "whence, *in general*, Dasein can draw those possibilities upon which it factically projects itself" (*SZ*, 383). The death-analysis provides no answer to this question. Projection upon death assures that Dasein's resolve will be its own and made in light of the totality of its Being, but it does not tell us anything about how Dasein resolves upon one course of action rather than others.

To meet this demand Heidegger turns to the notion of facticity, thrownness or having-been. The past provides the content or substance that allows Dasein to escape the arbitrariness of rootless resolve. If the death-analysis appeared to vest the individual with absolute moral authority, the account of historicality shifts the locus of authority onto the inherited and shared past: the heritage or tradition in which one's possibilities are always rooted. But this grounding is questionable. For the possibilities offered by my historical situation to become my "personal fate" I must not passively obey "the authority of the fathers" but rather must critically engage the tradition that has been handed down to me—and not from some higher standpoint *beyond* it, but rather *through* it. The process of reappropriating a heritage to which one has been appropriated—which is nothing less than the process of authentic education—means handing down *to oneself* the possibilities that have been handed down to one: thinking them through for oneself. But this precludes unquestioning conformity with the authority of the past.

Though Heidegger calls this critical reappropriation a "repetition" of one's heritage (*SZ*, 386), he does not mean an imitation of what has already been but rather a recovery of what is worth preserving and nourishing. This occurs by way of a conversation or "reciprocative rejoinder" (*SZ*, 386) with what has been given, so that one appreciates the opportunities one's tradition affords as well as the limitations it imposes. One confronts these limits from within the tensions and multiple meanings that any tradition embodies, not from a position radically outside the tradition. One moves toward the future in a visionary way not by leaping over the past but by understanding it better, so that one appreciates what is being left behind when one criticizes it for the sake of a better future.

Being-unto-death and historicality are intimately connected because Dasein's authentic affirmation of its mortality makes possibilities previously implicit in the historical situation explicit, and this means that Dasein has the possibility of dying not blindly but "*fatefully*" through an understanding of its commitment to what is urgent and compelling in its situation. That one's fate needs to be chosen through the critical repetition of one's heritage does not imply that one is absolutely free to constitute the meaning of one's historical situation *ex nihilo*. Fate is rooted in the facticity of the historical situation a person has inherited. But this does not imply historical determinism or fatalism either. Possibilities harbored within one's heritage must be disclosed or opened up by resolute Dasein lest one be tossed about by circumstances that seem entirely fortuitous and external to one's "subjectivity." Fate does not mean that the individual is a passive victim of circumstances but that only the resolute individual can seize upon possibilities that have been sent his way. How we understand ourselves changes the situation. To understand a situation as meaningless or hopeless leads to an inability to act. In his later writings on technology, Heidegger suggests that the destiny that guides us in our time is that we will be fate-less: unable to take hold of our own possibilities. Be that as it may, conscience calls not for a spontaneous and arbitrary self-assertion but for a thoughtful engagement with one's past so that what is worth carrying forward can become explicit in a "moment of vision" (*SZ*, 438).

Though Heidegger's notion of "the moment of vision" prompts us to recollect Plato's idea of an intellectual intuition of the Good, the phenomenon to which Heidegger points does not involve a knowing subject directed toward a metaphysical, transcendent object. In the moment of vision one "sees" what is to be done in light of the basic structure of human existence and the particular historical situation in which one finds oneself, but without recourse to a transcendent measure. Because the past one is called to appropriate is always a shared inheritance—*our* past—and the future toward which one projects oneself is a communal possibility—*our* future—one never speaks for oneself when one articulates a moment of vision; one speaks for "us." Dasein's historizing is always a co-historizing in and with its "generation." But because this vision is conditioned by the contingent circumstances which let one see things as one does, it is always prejudicial and so precarious. Though personal fate is guided in advance by the common heritage one shares with others, it is "only in communicating and struggling [that] the power of destiny becomes free" (*SZ,* 384).

Just as one only has a personal fate when one takes hold of the possibilities handed down to one and makes them one's own, so the community only has an authentic "destiny" when it is not just a collection of atomized fates but reappropriates its past through an ongoing conversation among its members. If "fate" signifies the way Dasein takes hold of itself through a resolute relationship to the events of its time, "destiny" signifies the essential connection between the individual and his community or people. Dasein's original *Mit-sein* manifests itself as a *Mitgeschehen.* The sense one's life can make—the meaning one can give to it—is deeply constrained by the communal narrative in which one's own story is embedded. And this communal narrative is tied to the specific memories and legends through which one's community retells its story so as to define and reinforce its own ideals and distinguish itself from other groups.

The fate of the individual is conditioned by the destiny in which he stands, for destiny is not a collection of atomized fates but "guides fate in advance" (*SZ,* 384). Yet it is only through authentically fateful individuals who have resolutely repeated their own heritage that the power of destiny is set free. Though the past conditions the range of one's possibilities, it is up to Dasein to make these possibilities explicit and incorporate them into its existence. This occurs in what Heidegger calls "a choice of one's hero" whereby one finds what is worthy in the past crystallized in an admirable precursor (*SZ,* 385). It should be noticed that the object of one's resolute decision is not a particular action or principle of action but rather an individual hero whose life and character *as a whole* one admires.

It is in virtue of one's sense of life as a whole that one is capable of authentic *Verstehen* or understanding. This capacity for judgment harks back to the classical notion of *phronesis*: the power to find the universal in concrete circumstances, to know what is demanded by the particular situation. This power presupposes not theoretical but practical insight, a condition for which is the experience of and feeling for the shape of life as a whole within the particular community to which one belongs. Authenticity lays down the conditions that make *phronesis* possible but it does not establish a single, universal standard or principle for proper conduct. The project of modern ethics—to posit a foundational decision-procedure that would render irrelevant the historical context in which judgment operates—is seen by Heidegger as distorting the way in which a historically situated, free individual can come to know what is to be done. Decision is not a matter of conforming to abstract rules but of insight into what is demanded by the historical situation when one has looked death in the eye.

The visionary individual does not impose a destiny on his community but articulates their sense of what is best in their past and persuades them to carry it forward. Authentic historicality precludes the determination of destiny either by the momentum of the past or by the will of the few. Heidegger's approval of Count von Yorck's claim that public education aimed at the cultivation of authentic individuality should be the pedagogical task of the state implies that the moment of vision is not an arbitrary self-assertion but rather is oriented toward the good of the community as a whole (*SZ*, 402). The authentic creator or leader wants autonomous respondents, not an obsequious or coerced herd. To demand authenticity of a person is to demand that he make what others have established "his own" and that he let others make what he has proposed "their own." This precludes any unquestioning obedience or totalitarian ruling.

Heidegger's rooting of Dasein in historicality challenges the evaluative nihilism implicit in the existentialist interpretation of authenticity. Since one's fate has social implications, its meaning is at once personal and communal. And nihilistic indifference is precluded because the choice of what is worthy in one's heritage is neither passive conformity nor rebellious self-assertion but rather includes an essential moment of criticism, implying that not all historical understandings are equally valid. But if fundamental ontology does not subordinate the process of criticism to any measure higher than what happens to prevail historically, doesn't the historicist interpretation simply resolve the problem of the existentialist reading—arbitrariness at the level of the individual—by replacing it with arbitrariness at the level of the group?

II

Charles Guignon claims that Heidegger's principle of historicality provides the process of criticism with a higher measure. Guignon interprets *Being and Time* as an attempt "to combat the 'groundlessness' of the contemporary world by uncovering enduring values and meanings within the framework of 'worldliness' and human finitude."[1] Heidegger's account of authentic historicality, contends Guignon, provides an immanent critique of the existentialist view that authenticity is solely a matter of personal self-determination, for historicality introduces a transpersonal dimension that "points towards a communal sense of responsibility for realizing goals implicit at the dawn of Western history."[2]

Guignon labels fundamental ontology "a foundational historicism" and traces this project back to the 1915 lecture on the concept of time in history in which Heidegger tries to show that "historiography is possible only on the assumption that history has a *telos* in certain basic values which weave past events into a meaningful, unified narrative."[3] Far from being a "nonfoundationalist," Heidegger, according to Guignon, reacts against the tendency of nineteenth-century historicists to see history as a series of disjunct, incommensurable epochs with no inner coherence, and instead develops through his entire corpus a "foundationalist" vision of history as "a unified totality filled with significance," a "coherent whole" united by "trans-historical meanings." The aim of the question of Being, asserts Guignon, is to restore a sense of "the gravity and responsibility of existence" by recovering a more profound grasp of what it is to be. And this obligation receives its directive from Dasein's retrieval of "the enduring ideals and aims" of its heritage: goals that lie beneath the crust of tradition in a "most primordial," "original" relation to Being that provides "guidelines for all understanding and interpretation."[4]

Guignon's Heidegger stands Hegel on his head. History possesses a kernel of meaning that is present from the very beginning but this seed does not develop through time by rational necessity. Instead the history of metaphysics encrusts this kernel in a shell that must be cracked if the fruit is to flourish. Rather than assuming that historical time is the story of the maturation and elaboration of the original core of meaning, Guignon's Heidegger reads history as process of construction that conceals this primal source, a process that must be "de-constructed" if we are to trace back to the *arche* that provides history with its *telos* and guiding thread. Authenticity demands that we take over our indebtedness to the historical past in "the appropriate way" by appreciating how the key "elemental words" by which we expressed our Being-in-the-world from the very beginning have been leveled down through history and especially by modernity's unstable alliance between materialism and existentialism, objectivism and subjectivism.[5]

Guignon is surely correct that Heidegger's account of historicality calls into question the existentialist interpretation of authenticity, for the temporality of individual existence is always bound up with the concrete history of the particular, ongoing culture to which one belongs. When Dasein's dependence on and indebtedness to the wider cultural context in which it finds itself is overlooked, "it is natural to see the concept of authenticity as referring to a life encapsulated in a shell of personal commitments without concrete content."[6] Then authentic freedom appears, in words by which Philip Rieff describes "the triumph of the therapeutic" in contemporary life, as "a way of using all commitments which amounts to a loyalty to none."[7]

Guignon's position is problematic, however, because the point of Heidegger's appeal to historicality—that the content of one's possibilities derives from the particular heritage to which one belongs—casts doubt upon the assertion that there are enduring, transhistorical meanings that unify history in a single, coherent *whole*, or *an* appropriate way of interpreting the past, or a single *past* that we have to interpret, or a single "*we*" in the position of interpreting "*the*" past. Heidegger's affirmation of "the hermeneutical circle" implies that one's perspective on the past is always rooted in the particular heritage one already belongs to and that there is no way of overcoming the limitations and opportunities afforded by one's time and place to get a pure glimpse at Being or to attain an "original" and "most primordial" relationship to Being. The pretense of believing that one can respond to Being in "*the* most appropriate way" would be regarded by Heidegger as a vestige of metaphysics; instead, an awareness of our historicality lets us recognize that all disclosure is accompanied by "concealment" because there is no aperspectival understanding or interpretation.

Guignon's claim that the aim of the question of Being is to uncover *enduring* and *transhistorical* meanings, values, goals, and ideals that were present in a most *primordial* relation between Dasein and Being sounds too antihistorical and metaphysical, and does not accord with Heidegger's own criticism of the philosophical appeal to transhistorical foundations in ethics. Even if the structure of historicality itself is transhistorical in the sense that it is constitutive of the ontological structure of Dasein's existence, this structure does not furnish Dasein with an objective foundation, fixed yardstick, or neutral metalanguage for assessing rival self-interpretations or spiritual outlooks; it only establishes the site wherein Dasein is called to appropriate its own existence. Authentic historicality demands that Dasein be explicitly thoughtful about its time and place, but this does not enable Dasein to rise above the contingencies of history—only to be more aware of the prejudices that necessarily guide one's understanding and interpretation of the past.

When Heidegger states that the past—"the repeatable possibilities of existence"—should be revered as "the sole authority a free existing can have" (*SZ*, 391), he does not mean, contra Guignon, that history is the source of transhistorical values that provide permanent guidelines for all understanding and interpretation. Rather than being a foundation for enduring goals, the past provides an ever-changing context within which the projection of goals takes place. In this regard it is more appropriate to call history "an-archic." The lesson of our historicality is that the search for a pure origin that would provide a single overarching goal weaving history into a single, coherent whole is futile. Though the manner in which we as members of a heritage "stretch along" from past to future gives our lives a "connectedness"—a continuity that was missing when Being-in-the-world was analyzed simply in terms of personal temporality—this connectedness is not forged by imitating a transcendent measure, but must be perpetually reestablished in light of the uniqueness of the present situation.

But if fundamental ontology does not, and is not intended to, ground human existence in transhistorical values and meanings, does this imply that it is just another version of the very "historicism" that Guignon claims Heidegger intends to overcome through an inquiry into Being? If the framework of worldliness and finitude that *Being and Time* discloses does not sustain but rather subverts the "onto-theological" project of securing ourselves by reference to a permanent *telos* underlying our history, then it would appear that fundamental ontology does not "combat the 'groundlessness' of the contemporary world," but is just another symptom of "the death of God," of the absence of an enduring ethical measure. "Historicism," on Guignon's interpretation, is the view that values and meanings are inevitably expressions of particular historical contexts and so there is no common and permanent measure before which different versions of our ideals and goals can be judged. Historicism implies nihilistic relativism, and the refutation of it demands nothing less than the vindication of the traditional "onto-theological" project. If fundamental ontology cannot meet this high standard, Guignon worries, then it must fall prey to the very disease it was supposed to cure. Fundamental ontology would not be a "foundational historicism" but just plain historicism.

Emil Fackenheim agrees with Guignon that "the doctrine of historicity" at the heart of *Being and Time* poses a challenge to "historicism," but Fackenheim defines historicism differently and also provides a different account of the sort of foundation or ground that Heidegger's antihistoricist project offers.[8] Historicism, according to Fackenheim, is the view that all philosophical questions are superseded by historical ones. If human being is a project of self-making, then all its activities, including philosophy, must be historically influenced constructions. But the advocate of historicism is committed in spite of himself to a transhistorical metaphysical insight, one that cannot be proven on empirical grounds: namely, *that* human being is a historically situated self-making.[9]

The doctrine of historicity distinguishes itself from historicism, according to Fackenheim, by admitting this moment of self-recognition. All acts of self-making may be historically situated *except* the act by which historically situated self-making recognizes itself as such. Fackenheim claims that the early Heidegger repudiates historicism precisely by defining the structure of historicity as the essential character of the human situation. Unless fundamental ontology is to subvert its own ontological claims, it must allow for a moment in which thoughtful Dasein can rise above the particularity of its circumstances and grasp the essential structure that governs human existence in all times and places. This structure is not produced by Dasein but is the prior condition of all its projects.

If one can say that Dasein is the form of existence in which each individual participates and which it is up to each individual to make his own, then Heidegger's project has a "Platonic" dimension. But Dasein does not transcend its own particular cultural horizon toward "the Good": an encompassing metaphysical horizon that would provide it with a permanent *measure* against which to judge the practices of its time and place. Rather, Dasein can transcend its average everydayness, grasp itself as a whole bounded by nothing other than the temporal and historical structure of its own existence, and so be brought back to the conditions granted by its own finitude. Transcendence lets Dasein recognize itself for what it is as a whole but not to escape from the limits imposed by the facticity into which it is thrown.

Even if one grants that Heidegger's "doctrine of historicity" meets the problem of historicism as Fackenheim defines it, the doctrine leaves unresolved Guignon's worry about evaluative nihilism. Although the doctrine of historicity requires an appeal to a transhistorical moment in which the philosopher rises above his particular circumstances and comprehends the ontological structure of Being-in-the-world *as* "historically situated self-making," this version of the transhistorical and of the ground or foundation it provides does not protect the doctrine of historicity from the charge of historicism in the sense of evaluative nihilism. The ontological insight that we are a "stretching along" between past and future and so are subject to both compulsion and freedom does not provide us with any directive as to how to appropriate the past. The content for decision inevitably comes from the heritage in which we stand and so cannot be divorced from the *ontic* or *existentiell* dimension. At the level of the *ontological* all that is revealed is the human situation in general: the structural context that places us and through which all possibilities open up. Fundamental ontology combats the existentialist version of nihilism—that we live in sheer groundlessness—by articulating the transhistorical essence or ground of the historical situation to which we belong: the always prior basis of our projects. But this ground remains groundless in the sense that it does not provide transhistorical values and meanings but only the context of finitude and worldliness within which we appropriate historically conditioned possibilities.

This context *of* meaning does not provide a permanent set of *meanings* that would let us understand our history as a single narrative. The ontological analysis cannot arrogate to itself a decision-making power about ontic possibilities; it can only encourage a decisiveness in the making of decisions. In light of this Fackenheim asks, "Must not historicity fragment human history into a multitude of individual histories the scope of each of which does not transcend the limits of anticipated death, recollected memories and whatever commitments (or lack thereof) are situated between these?"[10]

III

The turn to the past as the measure of the future does not banish the specter of evaluative nihilism after all, for Heidegger fails to support his insistence that authentic historicality requires a *critical* reappropriation of one's heritage with an account of how such criticism is possible. From Heidegger's ontological analysis of historicality—his description of an understanding that involves a movement of repetition and rejoinder—nothing follows as to what the content of history ought to be. There is no basis on which the evaluative criteria necessary for substantive criticism can be derived from the ontological conditions of historicality. Suppose that a community is faced, as it always is, with a plurality of conflicting "moments of vision." These perspectives are not self-validating. The problem is to make sense of the activity of judging which is truer or better. That each vision contains elements of self-criticism is not enough; for criticism to have persuasive force, there must be reason to believe that the critical account is true, not false or arbitrary. Unless more can be said about what makes good judgment possible, the danger of evaluative nihilism has not been defeated by the appeal to historicality.

Ernst Tugendhat points out how ironic it is that authentic choice is supposed to bring Dasein back from its lostness in the arbitrariness and contingency of the possibilities in which it actually finds itself.[11] Such a choice requires a standard, yet Dasein does not possess a material standard which it would merely have to apply to its possibilities like a fixed yardstick. A standard, therefore, can only mean *a way of confronting one's possibilities*: a manner of raising questions about them. Heidegger offers as his standard our confrontation with death. But even he admits that anticipation in the face of Being-unto-death, though a necessary aspect of the standard for authentic choice, is not sufficient. And so he refers us to resoluteness in the face of our historical thrownness to supplement anticipation and to provide it with content. But this casts his concept of authentic choice into a vicious circle. On the one hand, choice is supposed to free one from the contingencies of the historical possibilities in which one actually finds oneself. On the other hand, choice is rooted in historicity, in the possibilities in which one actually finds oneself. But to say that the possibilities to be chosen are those that are in fact given provides no criterion for choice *among* possibilities. Authenticity, therefore, collapses into irrational decision.

Authentic historicality falls prey to the very arbitrariness that threatened authentic Being-unto-death, for unless the resolute choice of one's hero and the moment of vision are based on a recognition of what is really worth repeating in the past and are part of a commitment to persuade others of the validity of one's judgment, we are left with an array of conflicting assertions with no ground for choosing reasonably among them. If the discussion of historicality shifts the onus of moral authority from the individual to the past, the question still remains "How do I know what is worth repeating in what has been handed down to us?" If authentic historicality is to be more than a slavish obedience to the authority of previous generations, then there must be something about the present individual and his situation that lets him recognize in the past or the heroic precursor's stance the measure of his own. If there is no measure in virtue of which an individual can judge for himself whether the communal destiny that leaders of the community call him to subordinate himself to is legitimate, then the rooting of resolve in the inherited past occurs by way of a sacrifice of the very freedom that is supposed to be at the heart of authenticity.

If there is nothing that lets the individual discern whether his heroic precursor's stance or his leader's work is more than an arbitrary or short-sighted establishment, then there is no way of distinguishing an authentic resolve to repeat or critically appropriate the past from a readiness to be seized by it. Karsten Harries contends that there is a tension between Heidegger's understanding of authenticity as a call to truth and his interpretation in "The Origin of the Work of Art" of the state as the work of a violent creator who is not subject to the laws because he creates them.[12] To demand authenticity of individuals is to demand that each make what others have established "his own." Though this rules out any unquestioning obedience or totalitarian ruling, it leaves open the question of how one is to discriminate truth from semblance, the genuine leader from his false counterpart.

Harries claims that what is missing in Heidegger's account of authenticity is the notion of "the *earth*": that which inevitably remains *concealed* by our aggressive effort to appropriate what is not ours and so gives direction to the search for truth. In his writings after 1935 Heidegger emphasizes that all human work must remain open to what has remained hidden, that in establishing a world our work must also preserve the earth. If "the world" represents what we have established and accepted, what we take for granted in what has been transmitted to us, "the earth" embodies what is not transparent in our "conceptual scheme," but which immediately claims and moves us and subverts the security of what has been established and accepted. Once we recognize the finitude of any disclosure, we also acknowledge what it conceals. The world is grounded in the earth: an abyss or *Ab-grund*. Authenticity demands an openness to the earth, for all genuine work not only reestablishes a world but recalls us to the precariousness of what has been established. How we repeat the past is not arbitrary but it is always questionable because the possibility of error cannot be avoided. The earth remains the ever elusive measure of the prejudicial projections that constitute the world at any particular time and place. Heidegger's account of authenticity remains too "decisionistic" on Harries's reading, because there is nothing beyond the historical world we have projected to provide a measure for our projections and so to allow for the distinction between the genuine leader who presents a legitimate vision of where we are and his false imitator.

IV

Those who accuse fundamental ontology of being morally nihilistic con-
tend that Heidegger's image of authentic existence gives us no way of
discriminating between morally good and bad people and no basis for
preferring emancipatory over oppressive social practices. This is because
Heidegger allegedly fails to account for—or relegates to the level of
inauthenticity—the individual's awakening to the moral "weight" of the
lives of other persons. There is no reason why the authentic individual,
as Heidegger portrays him, would in principle condemn social policies—like those implemented by the Nazis—which deny that in fundamental moral matters everyone ought to count equally. If moralities are
ultimately the groundless constructions of individuals or groups, so the
argument goes, then the Resistance in World War II stood on no firmer
moral ground than the Brown Shirts. It was just a battle between two conflicting "myths" regarding the way things ought to be.

There are even those who go so far as to claim that the moral
nihilism of Heidegger's philosophy is responsible for—or at least helps
to explain—his vulnerability to Nazism.[13] This charge has three different
versions. The strongest one—advocated most recently and notoriously
by Victor Farias—is that fundamental ontology is a proto-Nazi doctrine.
The rhetoric of "historicity" sanctioning the fateful appropriation of
Being-unto-death and one's heritage and encouraging one "to choose
one's hero" bespeaks a nostalgic and authoritarian sensibility that leads
directly, according to this reading, to Heidegger's pro-Nazi speeches just
six years after the publication of *Being and Time.* In these Heidegger pro-
claims "the truth and greatness of National Socialism"—calling the
Führer "the reality and law of the German present and future"—and
announces that "Germany's student body is on the march" in "genuinely following" leaders who promise to create for its people its truly spiritual world, "the power that most deeply preserves the people's strengths,
which are tied to earth and blood."[14]

The weakest version is that Heidegger's philosophy is morally
flaccid and so offers no intellectual resistance to fascism. Ernst Tugendhat, for example, asserts, along the lines of Olafson, that Heidegger's
"derationalized" concepts of truth and choice turn *Being and Time* into a
manifesto of irrationalism or decisionism. The absence of the concept of
the good, of deliberation, and of the justification of normative judgments in fundamental ontology ultimately traces to Heidegger's idea
that the truth of existence is resoluteness. The primacy of resoluteness,
according to Tugendhat, "banishes reason" from human existence and

from the practical self-relation in particular by divorcing authenticity from "the genuine concept of truth": a concept that presupposes an objective basis of deliberation and justification prior to decision. Tugendhat claims that Heidegger's "irrationalism" makes his Nazism "no accidental affair," that "a direct path leads from Heidegger to Nazism."[15] If Heidegger is truly an irrationalist, however, it is hard to see how this leads him to Nazism rather than anywhere else, unless one assumes that Nazism was a reasonable ideology for an irrationalist to embrace. But it is not clear why an irrationalist would be reasonable. Tugendhat, I think, would do better to say that, insofar as fundamental ontology offers no objective basis for discriminating among morally better and worse options, it presents no intellectual obstacle to Nazism.

Richard Wolin forges a subtle, third way between the paths of Farias and Tugendhat. Against Farias's strong charge, Wolin denies that Nazism is "a necessary and inevitable outgrowth" of fundamental ontology.[16] The existential analytic is "sufficiently formal and abstract that it allows for a plurality of existentiell readings."[17] But contrary to Tugendhat's weaker view, Heidegger's project offers no mere "decisionism" either. For we must take seriously Heidegger's own admission to Karl Löwith in 1936 that the category of "historicity" in *Being and Time* provided the basis of his political engagement.[18] On Wolin's reading, "historicity" is less formalistic than is generally assumed, for Heidegger's delineation of it expresses a "conservative revolutionary" ideology that was "influential among the German mandarin intelligentsia in the middle to late 1920s."[19] Because this ideology condemned modern democracy, capitalism, and Bolshevism alike as symptoms of nihilistic rootlessness and stressed the need for the heroic individual to actively subordinate himself to a supraindividual historical destiny, Wolin concludes that Heidegger's "existential decision" for Nazism in 1933 is explicable not as a sheer leap of faith but as what Heidegger took to be the political actualization of authentic existence under his historical circumstances.

Though I concur with Wolin's analysis of the relationship between Heidegger's life and his work, it should be stressed that the account of historicity in *Being and Time* is resistant to dictatorial, racist, and collectivist ideas. First, Heidegger insists that a genuine leader or hero have the autonomous, not coerced, backing of his followers. As one of Heidegger's foremost students, Hannah Arendt, has emphasized, one should not confuse authority with the power to impose one's will by threat of force.[20] Genuine authority proves itself when those who follow grant their assent because they are persuaded that the leader knows what is best for them. This does not mean that Heidegger would advocate democracy as the best political form of association in all situations. In fact, in 1933 Heidegger is critical of the kind of democracy represented by the United States, seeing it as a symptom, along with Soviet communism, of "planetary technology" or "the universal will-to-power": an impulse to impose a homogeneous form of technical-administrative order on all of civilization and thereby to deprive particular cultures of their spiritual roots.[21] One might even say that Heidegger was prescient in his sensitivity to the imperialistic direction of the budding relationship between the global superpowers. But Heidegger's skepticism toward mass democracy should not be equated with support for fascism.

Second, Heidegger's emphasis on Dasein's freedom makes fundamental ontology resistant to any biological reductionism. Heidegger claims in retrospect that he never took the racist theories behind Hitler's ideology seriously: that he saw Nazism naively as an attempt to preserve German heritage against the leveling forces of "planetary technology." One can surely fault him for becoming involved with the Nazis in the first place and for breaking with them far too late and for reasons that attest to his penchant for totalizing speculation removed from the particular social realities at hand. But it is unfair to attribute this to a supposed tendency toward racism in *Being and Time* itself.

Finally, fundamental ontology surely allows us to condemn as inauthentic both Hitler's appeal to what was most herd-like in the German people and to the obsequious behavior of the common Germans under Nazism: their willingness to sacrifice their individuality for the sake of the collectivist fantasies of the *Führer*, their desperate need to believe in their own superiority, their desire to impose their will on those who differed and to exterminate those who reminded them of their own fragility. Nazism can surely be attacked in Heidegger's own terms as an inauthentic appropriation of the German cultural heritage, not as an aspiration toward an authentic "communal destiny."

But fundamental ontology remains vulnerable to the charge that its image of authentic existence is not sufficiently resistant to evil because it makes the very distinction between good and evil—and so moral responsibility—seem to be the by-product, rather than the precondition, of freedom. Though the opposition to Nazism gets some foothold in Heidegger's distinction between authenticity and inauthenticity, this foothold seems to be psychological rather than moral. Nazi ideology might be condemned not because of the effects its proposed policies would have on its victims, but for the self-evading manner in which Germans were taken in by such a perspective.

But unless one is willing to argue that murderous decisions or social policies *must* betray inauthenticity in those who endorse them, one cannot say for sure that murder is ruled out by the ideal of authenticity. Within the terms of fundamental ontology, one is only entitled to evaluate decisions by the extent to which they express the individual's having freely appropriated his possibilities: that is, on whether the individual has decided without relying on the impersonal criteria furnished by "the Anyone." But insofar as morality itself is one of the "illusions" of "the Anyone," one has no ontological basis for condemning murder on the grounds that it is evil; for the attempt to measure possibilities against an absolute, impersonal standard of good and evil is inauthentic. The only condemnation that can be made on ontological grounds is that one has chosen murder inauthentically. But it is horrifying to think that the judgment about murder should revolve around whether it was committed resolutely or not.

Only if one's moral liability to other persons is on an ontological par with one's responsibility to oneself—that is, only if the distinction between good and evil, based on one's primordial experience of the moral weight of others' lives, always already constitutes the essential human possibility and abomination of murder—do we have an ontological basis for speaking on behalf of the victims of murder. For otherwise they are only victims from within *some* conceptual scheme or contingent moral vocabulary, and all that is ultimately at stake is whether such a vocabulary has been adopted freely or slavishly by those who accept it.

V

The importance of the historicist reading of *Being and Time* is that it subverts the anarchism of the existentialist reading which places too much emphasis on the solitude of the individual facing his Being-unto-death. Only as a member of a community with a shared past does one seek to own up to one's fate in relation to a destiny "we" all face. But who is this "we"? If the ethical inadequacy of the existentialist interpretation of authentic dwelling is an atomistic individualism or subjectivism which fails to do justice to the historical community to which one belongs, the ethical danger of the historicist reading is provincialism or relativism. Instead of disconnected individuals, we are now faced with disconnected groups each of which defines its destiny within a particular, totalizing horizon. What especially troubles us is that in 1933 Heidegger believed Nazism to be the authentic communal destiny of the German people:

the legitimate reappropriation of the heritage to which he had been appropriated. If this is consistent with the meaning of authentic historicality in fundamental ontology, then even if it is a "fundamental ethics" in relation to the threat of a worldless subjectivism, the *ethos* it articulates has been purchased at the cost of any common measure that would enable a mediation among conflicting *ethoi* or of any responsibility to those whose voices are silenced, who are rendered marginal or "other," by the prejudices of a particular heritage. Who spoke for the Czechs in the Nazis' determination of "our" destiny? An inflated notion of shared heritage or destiny also obscures the extent to which individuals and subgroups within a particular community differ in their interpretations of who "we" are. Who spoke for the Jews in the Nazis' interpretation of what is most worthy in "our" German heritage? Not only does an overemphasis on the rootedness of a particular heritage risk locking out aliens who do not belong; it also risks locking in members who do not share the prevailing self-interpretations of the dominant group.

For whom do I speak when I say "we"? Do I have an obligation to include others as moral equals in my vision of "our destiny"? And what about those who do not belong to "our community," with whom I do not believe I share a common heritage? Can one find any authority in fundamental ontology for the moral imperative to treat all persons as ends-in-themselves—to include all human beings as rightful members of the most encompassing community, "the family of humankind"—or must this imperative be understood as just one among many possible historical interpretations of our destiny? If the latter is the case, then the cultural pluralism allowed for by the claim that our lives are historical through and through threatens to collapse into a relativism according to which there is no common ground or even minimal morality to which all human beings are subject simply by virtue of being human.

But is it fair to convict Heidegger on the charge that a "decisionism" infects his "factical ideal" of authenticity not only for the individual facing his mortality but also at the level of the group in the realization of its "communal destiny"? Though Heidegger made some regrettable, even despicable, choices in his life, it does not follow that his ontology of human existence is responsible for them or that authenticity is so devoid of content that it permits the appropriation of Nazism to count as an authentic repetition of possibilities latent in German heritage. But why not? The content of the choices one makes is an ontic matter so long as ontology only exhibits the conditions for the possibility of practical choice. If Heidegger's ontological analysis provides no guidelines except the imperative to be resolute, it appears to make room for any possibility whatsoever because it precludes none absolutely. Even if the individual is subordinate to a communal destiny, the notions of good and evil, right and wrong, to which he is subject have no transhistorical, cosmopolitan status but must be understood as historically specific idols of "our" tribe. On the historicist interpretation of *Being and Time,* there is no perspective independent of the heritage in which one stands—and the "prejudices" that govern it—to judge whether one set of idols or ideals is better than others.

Still, there is an important dimension of authenticity that is overlooked when one too quickly assumes that it is compatible with all "moralities," even those which involve using others "solely as means." Though Karsten Harries is correct in noting that Heidegger does not explicitly introduce the concept of "the earth" in *Being and Time* and so fails to allow for a measure of particular historical "worlds," one might argue that the earth is foreshadowed or implicitly present insofar as Heidegger recognizes that all "ontic" claims not only reveal but also conceal the Being of beings. To face up to the fact that our historical projection—our way of appropriating our heritage—is not *the* way, but just *one* way of approaching "what there is," is to honor "the ontological difference": that Being always exceeds the particular cultural horizon in which beings are framed "for us." This insight should render any particular repetition of the past precarious and open one to other possible lifeworlds and ways of encountering beings. Far from entailing a decisionistic closed-mindedness or dogmatism, authenticity would seem to encourage a self-critical skepticism: a recognition that since no resolution is absolutely warranted, one's own assertions should remain tentative and open to objections. While granting that there is no ahistorical standard for determining which objections are valid, it remains that one is subject to historically conditioned canons of rationality.

That authenticity demands an openness to the perspectives of others who resist inclusion in one's own claim about where "we" stand seems further entailed by the point that authenticity requires not only that each individual make what others have established "his own" but also that he permit others to make what he has established "their own." Heidegger suggests that a norm of reciprocal freedom, and so a moral orientation toward the other as an end-in-himself, is immanent in authenticity when he insists that

> Dasein's resoluteness towards itself is what first makes it possible to let
> the others who are with it "be" in their ownmost potentiality-for-Being,
> and to co-disclose this potentiality in the solicitude which leaps forth

and liberates. When Dasein is resolute, it can become the "conscience" of others. Only by authentically Being-their-Selves in resoluteness can people authentically be with one another—not by ambiguous and jealous stipulations and talkative fraternizing in "the Anyone" and what "anyone" wants to undertake. (SZ, 298)

To do justice to the ideal of authenticity as a whole one must focus on not only on Being-unto-death and historicality but also Being-with-Others. When one includes this third aspect in the picture, the possibility opens up that moral authority in *Being and Time* lies not only in the choosing individual and the inherited past but also in the freedom of others in the face of whom I own up to my own possibilities and whose existence is honored not when I subordinate them to my own needs but when I let them be free for their own possibilities. If an affirmation of one's own freedom involves an obligation to affirm the freedom of others, then authenticity cannot imply that everything is permitted, for it would rule out appropriations of one's heritage that clearly violate the justified demand of others that they be allowed to make what one has established their own rather than being coerced into a perspective in which they do not feel authentically included. Perhaps in authentic *Mitsein* as "liberating solicitude" we find the ultimate sense in which fundamental ontology is a fundamental ethics.

4

The Cosmopolitan Interpretation: Authentic Being-with-Others and the Authority of the Other Person

The existentialist reading of authenticity elaborated in chapter 2 fails to do justice to the moral life of the self because it portrays us as isolated individuals who lack any primal links or bonds with others. The historicist reading developed in chapter 3 is inadequate, too, because although it recognizes the individual as belonging to a shared heritage and community—what Hegel called *Sittlichkeit*—it places us in atomized, disconnected contexts and so fails to allow for the common moral ground Hegel called *Moralität*. If each community's destiny is specific to its time and place, then one worries that the larger world is composed of a plurality of provincial communities each of which is closed in on itself with its own particular moral self-understanding. Historicality does not account for how we move and mediate among different contexts, heritages, communities, or how we adjudicate among conflicting interpretations of our own community's destiny. It offers no account of the sense that *all* other human beings share in "our" destiny and that honoring this requires listening to the perspectives of others from beyond the horizon of my or our prejudices, of suspending our projections for the sake of others who may have been excluded.

But there appears to be a transhistorical and *cosmopolitan* dimension to *Being and Time* after all. The potential for authenticity is the defining character of existence. Even those whose historical contexts are very different from my or our own are centers of existence who transcend their immediate circumstances and interpret their lives for themselves. Does the recognition that not only my life but every person's existence is his own to lead make possible, and even obligatory, a particular kind of relationship to other persons? Perhaps an image of authentic community follows from the "factical ideal" of authentic individuality. If so, then this would provide a criterion for criticizing communities insofar as they fail to foster or live up to this potential.

To see whether such a measure is immanent in fundamental ontology, we must look more closely at Heidegger's discussion of Being-with-Others and especially at the phenomenon of "liberating solicitude" which he claims is made possible by an authentic self-relation. If Heidegger's insistence on the authority of tradition lends to his thought a "conservative" and relativistic cast, a "liberal" moment may emerge in the recognition of the claim of others who, from beyond "our" horizon, call into question the parochialism of our tradition insofar as it does not speak for them and who demand that we include their perspectives in the effort to understand ourselves. But is this cosmopolitan moment justified by the structures of fundamental ontology? Is there a way of accounting for the possibility that I am not only rooted in the heritage of the particular community to which I happen to belong but that an authentic self-relation allows me to feel, and even requires that I honor, a fundamental solidarity among fellow human beings? If so, this would suggest that the authentic individual possesses a kind of moral conscience: a feeling not only of self-responsibility but also of responsibility to others.

On the face of things, this suggestion conflicts with Heidegger's demotion of moral conscience to the status of inauthenticity. But perhaps there is a level of moral conscience more primordial than the one to which Heidegger refers when he claims that the morally conscientious person flees his particularity and escapes into "the security of the universal." The more primordial moral conscience of which I speak does not involve a subordination of self and others to a common standard that would provide a decision-procedure telling anyone what he ought to do in a particular situation; rather, it involves an attunement to the particularity of others, to others *as* truly other, stemming from an awareness of the singularity of one's own existence. Such an attunement would not evidence itself in a preoccupation with adopting an *impersonal* stance so as to apply without prejudice universal rules to particular circumstances; rather, it would manifest itself as an *interpersonal* orientation motivated by one's desire not to incorporate others into "the universal" but, rather, to "let others be" in their freedom for their own possibilities and to allow one's own self-understanding to be informed by theirs.

This kind of interpersonal relationship seems to be precisely what Heidegger describes under the name "liberating solicitude": an orientation toward others "made possible by" an authentic self-relation. We must explore the possibility that the individualizing power of anxiety—the mood that reveals the ultimate groundlessness of one's own existence—does not thrust authentic Dasein "beyond good and evil" but is the basis for a correlative mood that discloses the dignity of others in their struggles to "become who they are." If the affirmation of solitude in authentic freedom-towards-death does not simply cut one off from others but enables one to feel solidarity with others in their "otherness," then the opposition between inauthenticity and authenticity should be construed not as a split between public Being-with-Others and private Being-for-Oneself but as a difference between two orientations toward social life. Whereas inauthenticity marks off the range of encounters between persons who are absorbed in worldly concerns that derive their significance from an anonymously constituted network of public practices, authenticity points toward a form of coexistence in which one remains attentive to others as centers of transcendence and possibility who are never subsumed by the public projects in which they happen to be absorbed.

If a "dialogical" interpretation of authenticity is justified, this would imply that an important group of Heidegger's critics—including Martin Buber, Karl Löwith, Emmanuel Levinas, and Michael Theunissen—overlook a crucial, if understated, dimension of his "factical ideal" when they charge that his authentic individual is incapable of a genuine I-Thou relationship because the "I-myself" is ultimately in monologue with itself to the exclusion of others.[1] But does the *possibility* of liberating solicitude mean that "individualized Dasein" stands in an *essential* relationship to others? Does the other as a possible "object" of liberating solicitude imply that she, just by virtue of being human, makes a moral claim on my freedom?

II

Those who criticize Heidegger's portrait of authentic existence for its failure to do justice to the depth of the individual's connection to other persons appear to be confirmed in their judgment when we look at a passage of such importance that it is one of only two places in *Being and Time* where Heidegger emphasizes a phrase in bold letters. He summarizes authentic Being-towards-death as follows:

> *anticipation reveals to Dasein its lostness in "the Anyone," and brings it face to face with the possibility of being itself, primarily unsupported by concernful solicitude, but of being itself, rather, in an impassioned* **freedom towards death**—*a freedom which has been released from the Illusions of "the Anyone," and which is factical, certain of itself and anxious.* (SZ, 266)

That authentic Dasein facing its life as a whole is "primarily unsupported by concernful solicitude" suggests that such a character is a solitary individual who stands apart from, rather than being a part of, society. At this level, the Being-with-Others by which one ordinarily takes one's bearings and from which one derives so much of one's self-identity drops out and fails to provide support. When Dasein confronts "the truth of its existence," it faces itself alone, liberated from the comfort and security of being at home and of knowing its place in "the Anyone." It is a particular mood—anxiety—that individuates Dasein by casting it into a "nonrelational" encounter with its "ownmost" possibility: Being-towards-death.

Heidegger insists in the starkest terms that anxiety shatters the public character of average everydayness and leaves one without a familiar and shared context by which one knows what one is up to.

> In anxiety what is environmentally ready-to-hand sinks away, and so, in general, do entities within-the-world. The "world" can offer nothing more, and neither can the Dasein-with of others. Anxiety thus takes away from Dasein the possibility of understanding itself, as it falls, in terms of the "world" and the way things have been publicly interpreted. Anxiety throws Dasein back upon that which it is anxious about—its authentic potentiality-for-Being-in-the-world. Anxiety individualizes Dasein for its ownmost Being-in-the-world, which as something that understands, projects itself essentially upon possibilities. (SZ, 187)

One gets the impression that the authentic individual is in the world but not of the world, even that he has renounced the world or transcended it.

But precisely in the passages where Heidegger conveys this impression, he is quick to remind us that

> this existential 'solipsism' is so far from the displacement of putting an isolated subject-Thing into the innocuous emptiness of a worldless occurring, that in an extreme sense what it does is precisely to bring Dasein face to face with its world as world, and thus bring it face to face with itself as Being-in-the-world. (*SZ*, 188)

And just as "existential 'solipsism'" does not remove one from, but elicits a more intimate appreciation of the world to which one always belongs, so it does not detach one from, but places one in a new capacity for relation with others.

> [If] concern and solicitude fail us, this does not signify at all that these ways of Dasein have been cut off from its authentically Being-its-Self. As structures essential to Dasein's constitution, these have a share in *conditioning the possibility of any existence whatsoever*. Dasein is authentically itself only to the extent that, as concernful Being-alongside and solicitous Being-with, it projects itself upon its ownmost potentiality-for-Being rather than upon the possibility of "the Anyone." . . . As the non-relational possibility, death individualizes—but only in such a manner that, as the possibility which is not to be outstripped, it *makes Dasein, as Being-with, have some understanding of the potentiality-for-Being of others.* (*SZ*, 264, emphasis mine)

Though in authentic Being-unto-death one faces oneself alone without support from others, this does not isolate one from them but enables a kind of relationship to them—"liberating solicitude"—that is not available from within the posture of inauthenticity.

> Dasein's resoluteness towards itself is what first makes it possible to let the others who are with it 'be' in their ownmost potentiality-for-Being, and to co-disclose this potentiality in the solicitude which leaps forth and liberates. When Dasein is resolute, it can become the 'conscience' of others. *Only by authentically Being-their-Selves in resoluteness can people authentically be with one another*—not by ambiguous and jealous stipulations and talkative fraternizing in "the Anyone" and in what "anyone" wants to undertake. (*SZ* 298, emphasis mine)

Heidegger does not speak of authentic Dasein as being split off from inauthenticity but as involving a modification of the inauthentic. "Authentic existence is not something which floats above falling every-dayness; existentially, it is only a modified way in which such everyday-ness is seized upon" (SZ, 179). And "resolution does not withdraw itself from 'actuality,' but discovers first what is factically possible for it as its ownmost potentiality-for-Being in 'the Anyone'" (SZ, 299). It is clear that Heidegger sees authenticity as involving not resignation or a renuncia-tion of the world but rather a double movement of withdrawal and return, of disorientation and reorientation. In this return or reorienta-tion the world and others alike are disclosed in a new way.

> *Authentic* disclosedness modifies with equal primordiality both the way in which the "world" is discovered (and this is founded upon that dis-closedness) *and the way in which the Dasein-with of others is disclosed.* The "world" which is ready-to-hand does not become another one "in its content," nor does the circle of others get exchanged for a new one; but both one's Being towards the ready-to-hand understandingly and concernfully, and one's solicitous Being with others, are now given a definite character in terms of their ownmost potentiality-for-Being-their-Selves. (SZ, 297–98)

What remains unclear and needs to be considered is just how one's rela-tionships with other persons are altered by the individualization of the "Self." How does the affirmation of anxiety in the face of one's own finite freedom make the individual available to others in a new way?

What does Heidegger mean by "liberating solicitude," and why does this way of relating to others only become possible when one stands in an authentic relation to oneself? Liberating solicitude, writes Heideg-ger, "pertains essentially to authentic care—that is, to the existence of the other, not to a 'what' with which he is concerned; it helps the other to become transparent to himself *in* his care and to become *free for* it" (SZ, 122). Heidegger suggests here that to be preoccupied with the par-ticular matters with which another is concerned is inauthentic. This is because such solicitude takes for granted the projects in virtue of which the other is absorbed in the world and fails to draw attention to the free-dom in which the other's projection toward the future is itself rooted. To care not only about *what* the other is concerned with but, more funda-mentally, about the other's *existence* itself is to direct oneself toward the other's freedom for his own possibilities. Heidegger calls this "leaping ahead": "letting the other be" in his ultimately solitary responsibility for his own future or "to-be."

If "leaping ahead" means becoming "the conscience of another," what kind of relationship does this signify? What is it "to help the other become transparent to himself *in* his care and to become *free for* it"? We recall that one's own conscience calls one to one's guilt: to one's responsibility for taking hold of the circumstances of one's life and pulling oneself together even though one is not responsible for those circumstances in the first place. Though conscience *always* calls "the Anyone" to the "Self," one can "listen-away" if one does not want to have a conscience, if one is not *ready* for the anxiety that the call evokes. When I play the role of conscience for another, this must mean that I call the other to face his own anxious self-responsibility. I do not—in fact I steadfastly refuse to—take over for the other and thereby rob him of his task of choosing who he is to be without recourse to a neutral standard. As "his conscience" I must help to heighten his awareness that his possibilities are ultimately for him to resolve upon alone. But it would seem that one who leaps ahead on behalf of another cannot help the other *want* to have a conscience or be *ready* for anxiety any more than his own conscience itself can make him want to listen.

But is this to say that authentic Dasein stands in the *same* relationship to another as the other's own conscience does? If the other's own conscience is always calling anyway, what difference could it make that this call is supplemented by that of someone else? Another can play a special role in provoking one to listen and be ready for anxiety. We think, for example, of a relation between a good teacher and a student. The teacher's success lies not only in transmitting a certain subject matter but also in encouraging the student to think and question for himself and to disagree with the teacher if disagreement seems warranted. These traits will allow the student to eventually become a teacher in his own right. A mark of a good teacher is that he wants his students to be not obsequious disciples but independent partners in the search for truth. But the student might never develop his curiosity were it not for the provocations of the teacher whose own curiosity sets an example that his students admire.

Or we think of the relationship between therapist and patient. This is an especially complex situation because the inequality involved may be between adults. The patient comes to the therapist for help and so assumes that the therapist possesses a certain authority. But the success of therapy lies not so much in whether the patient's problems are solved—as if they are puzzles—but in whether the patient is able to work through the problems life inevitably creates on his own or with significant others in his life rather than with a paid professional. Still, were it not for the therapeutic relationship, the patient may never have been able to develop the self-respecting independence that is the mark of mental health.

Heidegger's distinction between leaping-in and leaping-ahead finds a parallel in Martin Buber's distinction between "imposing"—the way of the propagandist—and "unfolding"—the way of the educator or therapist. The good teacher or therapist cares for the other's becoming.[2] In "meeting" the other, the one who unfolds serves as a midwife to the birth of the other person's as-yet unlived life: unlived because the other has not yet discovered or developed "his own potential or actualizing forces." But unlike the "essential relations" of love and friendship in which a person does not just make his assistance available but opens himself to the other and hopes for mutuality—in which "one is not only concerned for the other but also anxious that the other be concerned for him"[3]—the pedagogical or therapeutic relationship in which one helps the other realize his own potential is neither conditional nor reciprocal. Whereas love and friendship are incomplete and will likely fall apart when affection is unrequited, the "way of unfolding" is to care in spite of—even because of—the other's rebellion, narcissism, depression, hostility, and mendacity. These traits reflect how much the other needs to be cared for. But the ultimate goal of this caring-for is to help the student or patient to better take care of himself. The relationships are not reciprocal because the student is not seeking to educate the teacher and the patient is not concerned for the welfare of the therapist.

In each case the threat to being the conscience of another lies in the temptation to "leap in" for the other's good, to assume too much responsibility for the other's welfare and thereby to deprive him of the freedom to determine and pursue his own possibilities. If being the conscience of another is a positive relationship, though, it must involve more than reminding the other of his freedom and then leaving him alone. But how can one help another *want* to be free any more than the other's own conscience can provoke a *readiness* for anxiety? Though Heidegger suggests that what we might call authentic communication is a special kind of conversation that is neither discussing some topic in particular nor discussing nothing at all, it is not clear what such communication involves.

I propose that being the conscience of another involves three moments. First, one must appreciate what the other gets out of listening-away and not owning up to anxiety. Second, one must also appreciate the price one pays for fleeing from one's self-responsibility. Third, one must help the other to see that the benefits of fleeing are not worth the costs, that losing oneself in "the Anyone" is self-defeating. By falling into the world and becoming fascinated with "the others," one "sells one's soul," to use an older language. What one avoids by taking one's bearings from the common expectations of "society" is the unsettling question: Who am I to be? To not live one's life in light of the responsibility this question entails is to have compromised the very freedom that makes one human because one finds this task too burdensome.

What does it mean that the aim of leaping-ahead is for the other to become "transparent to himself in his care" (*SZ*, 122)? Given Heidegger's critique of Descartes, it would be strange if he were claiming that the self has a privileged and certain relationship to its own representations, that its own experiences are clear to it even if what they are experiences of remains opaque. But Heidegger does not say that what is transparent are experiences, but rather that what reveals itself in conscience is the character of oneself as care. That I become transparent to myself does not mean that I "know myself" or have a hold on who I "really am." It means that I am in a position where my existence can be an issue for me, a position from which the question that is usually suppressed— "Who am I to be?"—comes to the fore.

But to be the conscience of another requires more than provoking the general question "Who am I to be?" in the soul of the other. As it stands this question is too abstract. A readiness-for-anxiety requires both a freedom for one's possibilities and an appropriation of one's thrownness. Resolve is not free-floating but is rooted in a thoughtful relation to one's past. To "think for oneself" or "work out one's problems on one's own" demands that one engage with the concrete situation one faces. Still, if the call of conscience is ultimately silent—refusing to inform one of just what one ought to do—then a silence or reticence must lie at the heart of authentic or existential communication, too. The one who leaps ahead must refuse to leap in, and not because, though he knows what is best for the other, it is up to the other to find and pursue this for himself, but rather because nothing is *objectively* best for the other and so it is up to the other to face this and resolve upon his life for himself. The authentic individual does not possess a third-person, neutral knowledge of what is best for the other but is able to pay attention to the other in his "otherness": that is, in his singular responsibility for taking hold of his own possibilities.

We are reminded here of Kierkegaard's notion of "indirect communication": that approach to another appropriate to the idea that "the truth of existence is subjectivity." Though Heidegger attacks the notion of subjectivity because it suggests that human beings are subjects who primarily stand over against an "objective" world which they represent to themselves rather than being in the world as the lived horizon of their involvements, it remains that for Heidegger the truth of existence is authenticity, and authenticity demands that one own up to the first-personal character of responsibility. To teach the other the truth of his existence is not to represent to him a proposition that calls for theoretical assent but to help him to assume responsibility for his existence insofar as it has no objective foundation or measure. We are reminded, too, of Nietzsche's new teacher who wants fellow free spirits or creators, unlike the old preachers, religious and metaphysical alike, who wanted to subordinate the herd to his Truth. The goal of authentic communication is not to get the other to abstract from his particularity so that he can follow the pure rationality of an argument but to lead the other to question and reflect upon the hypostatizing interpretations of the pale public world in such a way that he is freed to interpret the meaning of his existence for himself.

Isn't it by way of this kind of communication, rather than in the subordination of self and other alike to a universal moral law, that the other is treated most authentically as an end-in-himself? The point here is not that inauthentic Dasein is necessarily immoral, for moral conscience is itself an aspect of everydayness, but that only authentic Dasein is fully open to the other as a fellow "existence." Still, to care about the other's existence or freedom is to be distinguished from caring about the other's welfare; regard for another's welfare may be better served in some instances by "leaping in" on his behalf and taking over his possibilities for him. The object of liberating solicitude is not the other's good but rather the other's capacity for having an authentic relationship to his own existence, the other's freedom to determine his own good for himself. But unless regard for the other's *welfare* is *conditioned by* respect for his relationship to his own *existence*, a positive relationship to him betrays the paternalism characteristic of, and appropriate to, the responsibility of a parent for a young child or a caretaker for those who, by the misfortunes of nature or accident, cannot take care of themselves. It is one thing to leap in for the sake of the other's welfare in a particular instance, another to consider him incapable of taking care of himself. When one loses sight of the other's potential for authenticity, one subjects the other to a kind of humiliation in the guise of helping him. In this regard, it might be argued that leaping-ahead, even if it is not equivalent to acting out of concern for the other's welfare, constitutes the core of what it means to treat another as an *end-in-himself*. To be most deeply responsible to another person *as* other, as an individual who stands beyond the horizon of "the Anyone," I must be sensitive to the other in his potential for interpreting the meaning of his existence for himself.

If in leaping ahead the other person is revealed as an end-in-himself, then what Kant called "the kingdom of ends" would be rooted in an encounter of *reciprocal* or *mutual* leaping-ahead. Heidegger claims that the degree to which persons are "authentically bound together" is "determined by the manner in which their Dasein, each in its own way, has been taken hold of" in their devotion to a common cause (*SZ*, 122). When the participation of each comes out of his own freedom for himself and allows others their freedom for their own possibilities, then a shared project is authentic. We coexist authentically and so form an "authentic We" when each feels that he belongs to a common project yet encourages the others to pursue the project in a way that attests to their own individuality. This keeps the group from becoming a mere collectivity in which each must subordinate his own freedom in order to further shared ends. Every "authentic We" is fragile because it is composed of self-responsible members who live at the boundary of this membership. As Buber writes, "True community and true commonwealth will be realized only to the extent to which the Single Ones—out of whose responsible life the body politic is renewed—become real."[4] Individuation is not the enemy, but the condition, of our being "authentically bound together."

III

But Marjorie Grene, for one, contends that there is no room in fundamental ontology for authentic solidarity or for Dasein's treating another as an end-in-himself. She finds in Heidegger's portrait of authentic existence a streak of immoralism. What happens to the individual's relationship with others, she asks, when he resolves to be "not a mass of conventions but himself"? She notes that Heidegger says little about our Being-with-Others outside the conventional and inauthentic level of existence. At the level of authenticity, Heidegger focuses on Dasein's solitude. "*My* freedom is mine, and the awareness of it bears no intruders, for it is 'freedom unto death'; and from my loneliness in face of death no one can save me; nor can I, if I would, save or even pity another."[5] Grene admits that inauthentic Being-with-Others has an equivalent at the level of authentic existence though she calls it "a strange equivalent."

On the everyday level, *Fürsorge,* as distinct from my general togetherness with others, is my direct concern *for* them. It corresponds, for persons, to the care I give things—and one's everyday life consists generally of a combination of the two. Thus as a housekeeper I take care of the
pots and pans, floors and linens, but I also take care of my husband and
children. Or as an office worker I am concerned with files and
accounts, papers and typewriters, but also with employers and employ-
ees. This is all in the purely conventional, fraudulent mode of existence; and here, of course, neither I nor the others emerge as genuine
individuals but only as pseudo-centers in a pattern whose whole meaning is the distraction of the individual from his true nature. One might
then expect, at first glance, that, with the transformation of myself into
a genuine existence, I should also apprehend as genuine at least a few
of the others with whom I habitually deal, and that therewith my concern for them would become a concern for them as genuine, not merely distracted, centers of human history. But such is far from being the
case. I care for others in a genuine, rather than a conventional sense,
according to Heidegger, insofar as I refer my care for them essentially
and completely to my own free projection of myself. That is, in other
words, the contrary morality to Kant's: the free man is he who treats
other people always as means, never as ends. But such a relation is
hardly in any meaningful sense a togetherness of human beings or a
concern for them. Rather it is the debasement of others to mere tools
by the rare man of character who has risen to the level of a richer, genuine existence, who has resolved in ruthless independence to fashion a
life-toward-death, a freedom in finitude on his own pattern. A relation,
on the other hand, of concrete togetherness, in which two human
beings stand as free beings face to face—such a relation the single-
minded arrogance of Heidegger cannot envisage and could not toler-
ate.[6]

Grene reads Heidegger's conception of freedom as implying that the
authentic individual can only treat others as means, insofar as authentic
care for others is grounded not in the claim or demand that their rightful existence imposes on one but in one's own free projection of oneself.
If the moral responsibility awakened by the encounter with another person as an end-in-himself is experienced as a limitation on how one may
justifiably exercise one's freedom, as the obligation to be concerned for
the other's good *for his own sake,* then it would seem that this encounter
cannot be appreciated by a philosophy that traces the meaning of what
is other to the free projection of the self, to what is *for one's own sake.*

Does the *self-relatedness* of all care entail that Dasein is fundamentally *selfish* and unable to care for others for their own sake? How is *liberating* solicitude possible if care is always for *one's own* existence? Grene believes that "concern for others as genuine, not merely distracted, centers of history" is precluded by Heidegger's account of authenticity, because she presumes that regard for others as ends-in-themselves is not possible on the basis of a free projection of oneself. But isn't leaping-ahead precisely a relation in which I desire to be with the other as "two human beings standing as free beings face to face"? If authenticity makes leaping ahead possible, then the fact that care is always for my own being must, for Heidegger, be the condition of, rather than an obstacle to, letting others be free for themselves.

That care is inevitably self-related does not imply that it is selfish. That I can only be open to the other's horizon from my own, that my understanding of others is necessarily colored by my own prejudices, does not mean that I cannot learn from another. If the fact that one's own life-experiences are necessarily particular were a reason to mistrust them as means for understanding others, then one would be better able to understand others from the standpoint of utter naivete. But it is obvious that a naive standpoint, rather than giving one unprejudiced access to others, would leave one wholly without an orientation for understanding them. Though one's historical experience is always particular, it is not as if one would be better off trying to understand others in their "otherness" from some perfectly "universal" perspective or from no perspective at all. Heidegger suggests that one can only appreciate others in their potential for authenticity, and so as really other than oneself, when one affirms that one's own existence is one's own and so really other than "the Others." From the perspective of one's own uncanniness one can understand the uncanniness of others. This means that one does not incorporate others into the horizon of one's own determinations of who one is to be, but rather is able to let them be free to determine who they are to be for themselves.

If leaping-ahead is what it means to be responsible to another person as other, and if authenticity allows one to recognize others in this way, then it would appear that one's own authenticity is the condition for the possibility of treating others as ends-in-themselves in the deepest sense. But how is it that an authentic self-relation makes leaping-ahead possible? Why is it not possible for a person who exists inauthentically to "let the others be"? Heidegger's claim is that so long as I "listen-away" from my own "Self" I cannot listen to others. So long as I fail to heed the silent call of my own conscience and do not face my own possibilities apart from the ways of "the Anyone" I cannot hear the other apart from "the Others" either. To listen to the other in the most primordial sense is to hear not only what he has to say but also the freedom to which what he has to say ultimately traces.

It appears, then, that there is a correlation between my recognition of my own and others' freedom. I cannot face "I-myself" without acknowledging that other persons, insofar as they are "existences" like myself, are called to own up to themselves, too. That each of us can be "I-myself" means that our lives are defined by the same structure of care. But we are radically unlike one another, radically separated, in that it is up to each of us to come to terms with this structure for himself and to make of it what one will without appeal to a common measure. Leaping-ahead is possible because, though I acknowledge that the abyss the others face is the same as the abyss I face, our situations are absolutely incommensurate inasmuch as the abyss ultimately throws each of us back on himself alone. Leaping-ahead only becomes *desirable*, however, insofar as I see this aloneness, painful though it may be, as an important opportunity for the person "to become who he is." If anxiety were simply a negative experience, then perhaps it would be better for the authentic individual to shield himself and others from it.

Though authentic care for my own existence throws me back on myself, it frees me to encounter others in a way that is impossible within "the Anyone." Is it fair to say that out of the *solitude* of facing my own Being-unto-death emerges a *solidarity* with others in their task of becoming themselves? Though everyday life under the sway of "the Anyone" may betray cooperation in the pursuit of common goals, this cooperation falls short of authentic solidarity because it is not the activity of "an authentic We" whose destiny is determined by "struggle and communication among fateful, individualized Daseins" (*SZ*, 384). To whom does the authentic individual's feeling of solidarity extend? In fact one can only be actively involved in relations of liberating solicitude with very few. For the most part Dasein's encounters remain inauthentic. But it would seem that even inauthentic encounters are altered by the authentic individual's recognition that other persons are *possible* "objects" of liberating solicitude. The authentic individual is aware of the limitations of being with others in "the Anyone," aware of the extent to which the other in his individuality and "otherness" is forgotten in the course of "business as usual." This awareness makes the authentic individual sensitive to how even "moral" dealings with others fail to do full justice to them in their "existence." The question is: Does this sensitivity imply that the authentic individual possesses a conscience more demanding than what would ordinarily be considered "moral" because it is rooted in the imperative to treat others in a manner consistent with their having the potentiality for authenticity?

IV

Following the reading of J. Glenn Gray,[7] Frederick Elliston argues that it is a mistake to interpret liberating solicitude along moral lines. Authenticity, he insists, signifies genuineness in the sense of truth, not goodness. Liberating solicitude, a relation in which I desire another's authenticity, is not a moral relationship but an ontological one. The issue is not concern for the other's welfare but openness to the other's existence: care for the other as a being who is related to himself in such a way that he is called to "the truth of his existence." To be the conscience of another person is not to cast moral judgment upon him—to praise or blame him for acts of commission or omission or to remind him of "the right way to live"—but rather to call him to his existential guilt: to his responsibility for affirming his situation as his own and taking hold of his own possibilities. Because of its connection with truth as disclosure, leaping-ahead is not a moral ideal, though it does, Elliston claims, have "an *amoral evaluative component*."

> Different social encounters can make others more or less transparent to themselves, free them to varying degrees for their possibilities or entangle them partially or fully in their world. Judgments about these encounters are evaluations of the *degree* to which the Being of others has been revealed to them. But this evaluation is neither moral nor epistemological. Rather with his notion of truth as disclosure Heidegger is offering a new category for evaluations—an ontological one which cannot be reduced to any other kind.[8]

Unlike Marjorie Grene, Elliston recognizes that Heidegger allows for a relationship in which persons treat each other as more than mere means or tools: a relationship in which "two human beings stand as free beings face to face." Though Heidegger privileges leaping-ahead over other modes of solicitude, Elliston denies that this is a moral relationship. The focus of concern in leaping-ahead is not others' welfare but "the degree to which their Being is revealed to them": in Heidegger's terms, the degree to which their existence is "transparent to themselves."

According to Elliston, this is not the proper object of *moral* solicitude. To be the conscience of another is to be directed toward Being, not "the good": toward truth, not justice. Authenticity, even if it makes possible a "conscientious" orientation toward others that allows them to be revealed in the fullest sense of their Being as "ends-in-themselves," should not be mistaken for goodness.

William Richardson agrees with Gray and Elliston that we have no right to transpose the discourse of authenticity into the terms of morality. Heidegger, writes Richardson, "conceives his question about Being (and about man only insofar as man has a built-in comprehension of Being) as far more radical than any question about the 'oughtness' of human acts."[9] The question—What is man in his finitude?—is deeper than any moral question. Dasein's existential guilt expresses its ontological "indebtedness": its thrownness into, and responsibility for owning up to, the conditions of its finitude. Existential guilt does not itself found a moral obligation but is the prior condition which makes possible one's being an agent who can be subject to moral guilt.

Yet Richardson himself suggests that one might use Heideggerian structures to articulate a *non-Heideggerian experience.* In particular, Richardson claims that authenticity—"a free acquiescence to the finitude of truth which comes to pass through transcendence"—indicates "a possible new way of speaking about *conformity to moral law,* or more specifically to so-called 'natural' law, that would be correlative with the achievement of human liberty rather than a restriction of it." By "natural law" Richardson means "a law for man's action inscribed in his 'nature.'" He suggests that we may find the ingredients of "law-as-norm" in Heidegger's account of Dasein's "thrownness": "'Thrown,' Dasein is given over to itself to be. Truth (*aletheia*), therefore, though illuminated *through* Dasein, is nonetheless *given* to Dasein to accomplish through its gesture of free acceptance."[10] Richardson suggests that if the freedom of Dasein is itself the gift of Being, then Heidegger allows for a way of reconciling the autonomy of freedom with the alterity of its source. "Law would be *given* to Dasein as making claim to be accepted, but given as gift—gift precisely of original freedom to be freely *accepted* in authentic response."[11] If conscientious Dasein, in responding to itself, attests to a source that is other than itself, then the experience of conscience elaborated by Heidegger may give us a way of speaking about law-as-normative-command, "whereby the imperative character of the moral ought finds its foundation in the ecstatic nature of ek-sistence itself as drive-toward-Being."[12]

But it is not clear how Being grants freedom to Dasein in the form of a *moral* imperative. Even if conscience issues a demand that I conform to the truth of my existence, a demand that arises from a source that is not the effect of my freedom, it is not clear why Richardson supposes that this demand is that of a moral law. It is for this reason that Hans Jonas sarcastically, but nonetheless pointedly, states, with regard to Heidegger's later writing,

> It is hard to hear man hailed as "the shepherd of Being" when he has just so dismally failed to be his brother's keeper. The latter he is meant to be in the Bible. But the terrible anonymity of Heidegger's "Being," illicitly decked out with personal characters, blocks out the personal call. Not by the being of another person am I grasped but just by "Being"![13]

Unless the call of Being is a call not only to my own existence but also to the existence of *others*, my free acquiescence to the finitude of truth cannot be properly understood as conformity to the *moral* law. Even if existential conscience shows a structural similarity to moral conscience in that what one is called to respond to is not created by, but is constitutive of, freedom, the "object" of responsibility is fundamentally different in each case. Existential conscience calls one to care for *one's own* Being as a whole; moral conscience calls one to care for the existence of *others*. In the latter case, the source of the command is the Being of the other in his alterity even though the command can only be received by one who is free and so also capable of irresponsibility.

But why isn't the supposedly "non-Heideggerian experience" of conformity to the moral law implicit, if not explicit, in Heidegger's account of liberating solicitude? Why isn't leaping-ahead a form of goodness? Charles Sherover argues that, though Heidegger does not provide a full-blown moral philosophy, his categorial description of human existence does offer the outline of "an existential ethic." Sherover claims that Heidegger provides an existential foundation for Kantian liberalism insofar as a conscientious relationship to *one's own* existence—an affirmation of one's own freedom—yields a moral demand that one respect the free existence of *others*. The central thrust of Heidegger's project, according to Sherover, is "to ground and develop the Kantian thesis that all human reasoning is essentially of a practical nature."[14] Because the ground of practice is freedom, and freedom is always informed by a responsibility to others, human reasoning expresses itself most primordially in one's moral accountability to others for the exercise of one's freedom.

> Building on the fundamental Kantian distinction between persons and things, Heidegger has differentiated that circumspective *concern* we display to the things about us from our solicitous comportment toward other persons. Only through *solicitous* behavior do other persons enter into our experience as persons (instead of things). It is toward them that we are able to exhibit moral responsibility. Reminiscent of Kant's injunction that the prime responsibility is to treat them qua persons and to enhance their own free self-development, *Heidegger abjured the domination of others* because it infringes on their own sovereignty of care.[15]

Sherover overstates his case when he claims that solicitude *as such* allows others to enter into my experience as persons toward whom I have moral responsibility. First of all and most of the time, according to Heidegger, I encounter others as role-players in the public, workaday world, if I encounter them directly at all. Insofar as solicitude refers to the entire spectrum of ways I relate to other persons, as compared to my concern with things, it includes indifference, manipulation, and domination of all sorts as well as more benevolent engagements.

Sherover qualifies his point when he suggests that not solicitude in general but *liberating* solicitude in particular allows the other to appear as an individual capable of sovereignty over his own life. When I am open to the other in this way he appears from beyond the horizon of "the Anyone" as one over whom I ultimately have no sovereignty: as one whom I have *no right* to dominate. To appreciate that sovereignty is the essence of the other's existence is not just an ontological but also a moral recognition: that it is wrong prima facie to violate another's sovereignty. Against Elliston and Richardson, Sherover concludes that Heidegger's privileging of liberating solicitude is not an "amoral" evaluation but proof that individuation and moral responsibility go hand-in-hand. Referring to "leaping ahead" as that form of solicitude in which one shows concern for "the integrity of the other," Sherover claims that conscience demands that one make oneself responsible not only to oneself but also to "the free development of others."

The obligation to use freedom in a morally responsible way is, Sherover suggests, "rooted in the nature of freedom itself, in the heart of man's nature."[16] This obligation is, to borrow William Richardson's phrase, "a natural law": "a law for man's action inscribed in his 'nature.'" Heidegger has demonstrated the social nature of individuality, "the ontological primordiality of the sociality of the person," though admittedly he has left Being-with-Others "strangely bereft of any serious development." Still, he has said enough to rule out the moral nihilism of which he is so often accused, for he has shown that freedom carries with it a moral obligation to respect all persons as ends-in-themselves and a political obligation "to advance the freedom of the citizen under the aegis of a common good which can only be conceived as the social grounding of maximal individual freedoms."[17] The basis of political legitimacy is the mutually recognized freedom of the members of the polity. The existential basis of liberalism lies in the human capacity for morally responsible freedom—in the "ability to care about others as well as oneself" which "arises from any human perspective."[18] Moral liabilty is constitutive of, not constituted by, one's freedom.

Still, one has access to the other's integrity—his capacity to exercise sovereign care over his own existence—only by way of one's own sovereignty. Only through authenticity can I-myself relate to a Thou-self: that is, to a fellow I-myself whose task is, like mine, to take responsibility for himself. My sovereignty does not make me sovereign over others but issues a demand that I "abjure domination" and respect their own sovereignty. Sherover arrives at this conclusion because he regards the disclosure of the truth of existence to be the revelation not only of *my own* freedom but of freedom *as such*, of freedom as the core of every person's existence: "a person's ability to transcend the immediate confines of his momentary present, comprehend his wider present as a field of activity, discern the specific possibilities which by illuminating his present situation beckon him onward while yet retrieving the lessons requisite to his own chosen quest."[19] To respect oneself as a person is to respect the principle of personality as such: freedom or transcendence. On account of this, self-respect must include respect for others, and the acknowledgment of one's own freedom must produce a limit to the exercise of that freedom in one's responsibility, and so accountability, to others.

What is puzzling about Sherover's interpretation as a purported reading *of Heidegger* is that Heidegger never explicitly states that the *possibility* of liberating solicitude entails that the authentic individual has a moral *obligation* to honor the integrity and free development of others. Sherover goes so far as to suggest that the potential for authentic selfhood is not, as Heidegger states, the ontological condition for the possibility of experiencing moral guilt and conscience, but rather that authenticity itself is equivalent to a kind of moral responsibility to other persons that transcends the more ordinary duties one has toward others in the inauthentic public domain.

According to Heidegger, however, conscience calls me to *my own* freedom first of all; the silence of the call attests to the fact that no one can take my place when it comes to the task of existence, of leading my life. We are with Richardson in suggesting that a "moral" interpretation of authenticity requires using Heideggerian structures to articulate an experience—akin to what Kant calls "reverence for the moral law"—that is not described in, but is compatible with, fundamental ontology itself. The existential analogue to reverence for the moral law is the experience of the dignity of another human being. The source of the moral law, contra Richardson, is not Being but the other in his commanding alterity, even though the condition for response-ability to the other is a self for whom there can *be* an other or a "Thou." And what makes the experience of this source possible is the experience of one's own dignity. But can authenticity be equated with dignity so that the claim that an authentic self-relation makes liberating solicitude possible can be translated into the claim that respect for one's own dignity makes possible, and even obligatory, respect for the dignity of others? Is the acknowledgment of another's potential for *authenticity* the same as, or even related to, an appreciation of his *moral worth?*

V

I want to argue that regard for the other's potential for authenticity, though not exhaustive of concern for his well-being, is essential to respect for the other as a person whose dignity is lost when he is understood wholly from within the average, everyday horizon of "the Anyone." Insofar as the authentic individual understands himself as transcending the past—as standing in an eccentric relation to the taken-for-granted context of possibilities constituted anonymously by "the Anyone"—others are revealed to him as "fellow transcendences." This means that to do justice to them *as* others he must not treat them as if they are innerworldly entities within the horizon of his freely constituted possibilities or within a cultural network of practices, but must encounter them as independent centers of possibility in their own right: thrown into the same world as he is, yet transcending it just as he does. George Schrader contends that to encounter another person as "an existence" beyond the limitations imposed by cultural roles and stereotypes is to face a moral presence.

> If we were to accept the cultural situation as exhaustively determinative
> of human beings, we would be perfectly justified in treating some men

merely as slaves. Culturally viewed, such men might be said to be only slaves. Hence, responsible action would require only that I treat any one of them in a way appropriate to his station in life. A slave would be only a slave, a criminal a criminal, and an aristocrat an aristocrat. To live responsibly would be, as some people actually regard it, to treat each man in a way befitting his cultural situation. And this is, in fact, what conventional morality sanctions. It is, on this view, justifiable to abuse criminals, to exploit slaves, and to defer to the gentry. If we take into account only explicit or voiced claims, conventional morality is more or less satisfactory. But if we refuse to identify the *existence* of a man with the *role* he plays and refuse to deny that he is capable of transcending his appearance as a cultural object, we cannot be content with conventional morality. No man can be identical with his appearance in the way that a stone is simply a stone. To transcend oneself is an *a priori* characteristic of all human beings. . . . We are responsible toward others, then, not simply in terms of their empirical nature but, also, their existence. We are related to others in this twofold way and must take both factors into account if we are to act responsibly toward them. We are accountable to them even as we are accountable to ourselves.[20]

But how is it that the other in his Being as an existence or transcendence makes a moral claim on my freedom? If the claim of the other is constituted by my freedom *ex novo*, then we cannot explain the categorical nature of moral responsibility to others. But if the very acknowledgment of the other as being another person is the basis of his moral demand on me, it would seem that obligation coincides with freedom and, in addition, that this coincidence breaks down the barrier between facts and values, between ontology and morality. Schrader contends that this barrier ought not to be upheld because it is artificial.

It is the sheer *fact* of the other's existence in all its concreteness that constitutes the initial ground of our obligation to him. . . . His *claim* upon us derives from his totality as a person confronting us in our world. It constitutes a responsibility in the most literal meaning of that term, namely, as a liability for answering or responding to the reality of the other. At the point where moral reflection arises we begin to evaluate the legitimacy of claims which we attribute to the other or which he asserts for himself. We should not lose sight of the fact, however, that any possibility of a valid assessment of putative moral claims requires a reference to the concrete reality of the other in the context of our initial relatedness to him. If he is, in fact, a human subject, we are obligated to treat him as such and, hence, not "as a means merely." But, if so, the primary ground of the obligation lies in his person rather than in our own moral will. If so, it is *heteronomously* rather than *autonomously* grounded. . . . When we come to the point in reflection where we are capable of recognizing the other's claim and making it a principle of our action, we only countenance a liability antecedently given. . . . Kant's difficulty here stems from the fact that he confuses the *constitution* of a moral claim with its *recognition*. Our recognition of our duty to others first gives it moral significance for us. But the duty is categorical only because it derives from the undeniable fact of the other's existence.[21]

Is this a conflation of the ontological and the moral, or is it instead an insight: that the ontological here has a moral dimension? Even if we accept, against Elliston and Richardson, that leaping-ahead as the way of encountering another person most appropriate to his free existence may be construed as a primordially moral relation, it might be argued that the authentic individual cannot be expected to adopt a liberating posture toward everyone. For the most part the authentic individual continues to encounter others within the average, everyday world in terms of what they do or the roles that they play. Authenticity does not make all one's involvements authentic but is at best "a modification of inauthenticity." Still, it is plausible that one of the ways in which authenticity modifies inauthenticity is that one's own anxiety alerts one to the degree to which others are inadequately appreciated in the course of average everydayness. Even if I am not obligated to approach all other persons by *actually* helping them to be free for their own possibilities, I may be obligated to not treat others in a manner that is inconsistent with their *potential* for authenticity; that is, I ought to bear witness to the extent to which everydayness compromises their existence and fails to disclose them, in the deepest sense, "as they are." This is to suggest that the revelation of others' *Being* as "fellow existences" is not just an ontological disclosure but a moral *demand*.

But if others are only disclosed in their truth from within liberating solicitude, and this way of Being-with-Others is a rare phenomenon, how can all other persons, just in virtue of being "fellow existences," make a moral demand on authentic Dasein? One might reply that authentic Dasein need not *actually* leap ahead of another in order to acknowledge that the other, as a fellow Dasein, is one who *could* be approached in a "liberating" way. It might be objected, however, that even if authenticity makes it *possible* for individuated Dasein to treat others as "objects" of liberating solicitude this does not impose upon the authentic individual an *obligation* to treat others in any way in particular. If leaping-ahead simply describes a possibility for authentic Dasein, it by no means precludes the other possible modes of solicitude available to one who is inauthentic. Authenticity simply makes possible one more way of encountering others.

But doesn't the capacity to encounter others in their potential for authenticity affect the way one actually encounters them even in the course of average everydayness? The suggestion here is that the recognition that another is one whom I *could* encounter in the mode of liberating solicitude implies not that I *am* obligated to be the conscience of the other and leap ahead of him, but that I am obligated to act toward him in ways *consistent with the possibility of being his conscience.* And this means according him the respect owed to an individual who is free and an end-in-himself. There are ways of treating another that are not only inauthentic but also incompatible with the other's being one who is capable of authenticity. It is here that the authentic individual knows the line must be drawn. That the other is one who is free because his possibilities are his own to appropriate means that it is a violation of his "existence" to treat him as a pawn of one's own freedom. This suggests that the authentic individual is, on the basis of the experience at the heart of authenticity itself, subject to the imperative never to treat another person solely as a means. In keeping with Schrader's contention that freedom is the condition, but not the source, of moral obligation, Paul Ricoeur writes,

> The recognition of another freedom, the position of the other as having as much value as I have, are primitive acts which can be derived from nothing else. Why should we not kill if it were useful, reinforcing? Here is the fundamental limit of any technology of behavior, since it cannot take into account the notion of a person as "an end in itself" which is constitutive of the concept of dignity. To have a value and not a price, that is to have dignity, according to Kant. But the position of the ethical problem on the basis of the second person is a denial of the illusion of lawless freedom. Ethical freedom is not a claim which proceeds from me and is opposed to any control; it is rather a demand which is addressed to me and proceeds from the other: allow me to exist in front of you as your equal! Dignity is the demand of freedom at the second-person level. There would be no question of treating the person in myself as an end in itself, if I did not meet this requirement with reference to the other. In that sense, I am my own neighbor,

> because I am the neighbor of my neighbors. Therefore, freedom is no longer an extension of my attempt to escape control or avoid constraint. It is an extension of my recognition of the equal right of the other to exist.[22]

Though one need not actually be the conscience of every other in that one cannot actively appreciate and encourage everyone's freedom, one stands in a conscientious relationship to every other insofar as their very existence imposes a limiting claim on one's freedom. One's access to the other as what Marjorie Grene calls "a genuine, and not merely distracted, center of human history" makes a demand that constitutes one's "freedom for one's own possibilities" as *always already morally responsible freedom*, and so not only as self-responsibility but also as responsibility to others.

Heidegger casts a positive judgment upon leaping-ahead not only because of "the degree to which the Being of others has been revealed *to them*," as Sherover contends, but also because of the extent to which their Being has been revealed truthfully *to oneself.* Only on the basis of my leaping-ahead is the other person transparent to me for "who he is" in his totality: that is, as situated yet self-responsible freedom-unto-death. The disclosure of the other person's existence "in its truth" has moral implications for the one to whom the other's Being is revealed in this way, because it is the disclosure of a fellow existence to whom one is answerable.

The ontological question—What is man in his finitude?—cannot be separated from, or held to be prior to, "any moral question," Richardson notwithstanding, if it is the case that "man in his finitude" is essentially defined by his being morally accountable to others. My existence is rendered finite not only by my thrownness into a particular cultural and biographical context and unto death, but also by the way my possibilities are conditioned by the presence of others over whom I have the power of life-or-death. The description of moral responsibility as an ontological dimension of the care-structure need not preempt the existential issue— Who am I to be?—so long as the fact that my freedom is always already conditioned by my obligation to others does not let me escape my singular responsibility for making something of my life as a whole. Moral conscience is a primordial, not derivative, phenomenon because the free individual is, from the start, *answerable* to other persons for the effects of his choices on their well-being.

VI

So far, the bond between the authentic individual and other persons has been described in the language of obligation. The authentic individual, we have suggested, experiences others as making a moral claim upon him just in virtue of their being sovereign persons like, and yet radically other than, himself. His awareness of his freedom for his own possibilities coincides with an awareness of the limits of the rightful exercise of that freedom. These limits are the antecedently given conditions, not the effects, of freedom. I have no choice over my moral liability to others—my obligation to respect their dignity as fellow persons—though I do have the freedom to honor or violate my responsibility. I am already answerable to others for how I appropriate my own freedom-unto-death, at least to the extent that my choices impinge on their well-being.

But is there anything in the experience of anxiety that makes one aware not only of a duty toward others but also of a deeper, more heartfelt solidarity with them? The discourse of duty suggests that the morally responsible person is divided within himself: torn between what he wants to do and what he knows he ought to do. For Kant, an obligatory act is only morally praiseworthy if the agent performs his duty while wanting to do otherwise. Only one who rises above temptation in order to act rationally deserves praise. If the right deed comes too naturally, we do not applaud the agent's will because there was no pull to do otherwise.

Does an authentic affirmation of Being-unto-death allow for a way of Being-with-Others that heals this rift between obligation and desire? Werner Marx, who took over Heidegger's chair at Freiburg in 1976, suggests that the experience of mortality nourishes moral life because the unsettling and dislocating character of anxiety in the face of death gives way to a healing whose expressions are compassion, love, and mutual recognition.[23] By taking a Heideggerian experience in a non-Heideggerian direction—by finding in anxiety the root of compassion—Marx bridges the gap between solitude and solidarity. He sees in the shift from inauthenticity to authenticity a moral transformation from an attitude of indifference to one of appreciation.

The transformation takes place in three stages. Average everydayness—the first stage, in which one is absorbed in the familiar context of business-as-usual—is characterized by tranquillity, security, and a sense of permanence about one's Being. In taking one's existence for granted as "given and present without further ado," one adopts an attitude of "tranquilized indifference" toward one's own Being: an attitude that corresponds with an indifference toward others, too. One is propelled into the second stage—dislocation—by the anticipation of death, for it divests one of the illusion that existence is secure and permanent. Feeling displaced, isolated, and helpless, one turns to others for support and strength in one's "hour of need." Having owned up to the insecurity, impermanence, fragility, vulnerability, and dependence that pervade one's Being, one is able to seek compassion from others. In the third and ultimate stage, one identifies with others as sharers in the same tenuous and uncertain fate—one meets others as "brothers in the same darkness"—and so turns to them with compassion in their struggle to face honestly the insecurity and groundlessness of mortal existence. This, according to Marx, is the healing moment.

One knows the difference between good and evil from within because one has depended on others' willingness to help at times when others could have easily taken advantage of one's weakness. And one prefers good over evil insofar as one recognizes in others' neediness and vulnerability not an opportunity to assert one's difference from and domination over them, but rather one's identification with their condition as one's own, too. The experience of mortality provides a this-worldly norm or measure for responsible human action: a phenomenological basis for the difference between good and evil and for the preference for good over evil. The root of most evil, Marx seems to say, is not hatred but indifference: an attitude whose basis is the illusion, reinforced by the familiar routines of everyday life, that existence is not transient, contingent, and finite but rather permanent, necessary, and boundless. So long as we protect ourselves from the unsettling awareness of our fragility, we remain confident that our lives are on the right track and we tend to take credit for it, too, as if good fortune is the reward for superior character or effort. And we tend to put down or disregard those who are less fortunate than ourselves as if, perhaps, they deserve it; for to face the fact that our own condition is just an accident away from theirs would be too disconcerting and humbling.

To honestly accept our mortality, on Marx's interpretation, is to undergo nothing less than a moral conversion. When the indifference of average everydayness is shattered by the displacing and isolating power of death, the rift between self and others can be healed by the recognition that we are all trying to forge meaningful lives for ourselves under conditions that always threaten to undermine meaning and reduce our highest aspirations to nothing. Out of the memory that we were all once children who depended on the kindness of strangers in order to grow up and attain the illusion of adult self-sufficiency, and out of anticipation that we can easily find ourselves as helpless as children again, we can be moved to treat others compassionately. The mood that Heidegger focuses on—anxiety—though it does isolate the individual and thrust him into a "nonrelational" encounter with his own possibilities, also makes possible a mood that counters the superficial or indifferent sociality of everyday life: the morally disclosive mood of compassion which awakens one to the preciousness of existence, to the thin thread that separates accomplishment from failure, satisfaction from suffering, life from death.

If Marx is right, then an interpretation of authenticity that places emphasis on the self-sufficiency and sovereignty of the resolute individual who no longer sees himself in terms of "the Others'" expectations should be supplemented by an interpretation that stresses the appreciation of vulnerability and interdependence of one who is attuned to the fragility of Being-in-the-world. And the meaning of "liberating solicitude" should be altered accordingly. For when liberating solicitude means not only respect for the other in his effort to attain sovereignty over his own life but also compassion for the other given that freedom is always grounded in conditions over which he has little, if any, control, "being the conscience of the other" means not only helping the other to be free for his own possibilities but also helping him in "his hour of need." There is always the danger that compassion will lead one to leap in and dominate the other's concerns in the name of his welfare. But there is also the danger that "leaping ahead"—or letting the other be—may be a form of indifference to his concrete needs.

Martin Buber objects that authentic Being-with, as Heidegger portrays it, is not "an essential relation" between persons but "*mere* solicitude."[24] Though the authentic individual is concerned for the other, he does not care whether the other is concerned for him in return. He is not worried about mutuality because a sovereign existence is self-sufficient. Even while reaching out to help the other be free for his own possibilities, the authentic individual "remains within himself" because he makes his assistance, but not *himself*, accessible. "Self-being," freedom *for one's own* possibilities—the ultimate that Heidegger's individual is able to reach according to Buber—means freedom *from others*. Insofar as liberating solicitude allows one to let others be free *for themselves*, it implies, in effect, freeing them *from oneself*. One seeks to help the other be as self-possessed, as sovereign, as one already is. The individual does not need or depend on others to be authentic. Even if individuation makes it possible for one to be with others in a new way, they do not enter essentially into the constitution of one's authentic existence. Though Buber admits that a moral ideal of respect for each other's sovereignty may be taken to follow from the "factical ideal" of authenticity, this comes to what Michael Theunissen calls "*reciprocal segregation*" and so falls short of Buber's ideal of an essential, interdependent relationship between self and others. According to Theunissen:

> Letting be, which, from a positive standpoint, stands for the recognition of the ownmost being of others, is, from a negative standpoint, the dissolution of all direct connection between others and me. Others can only be freed *for themselves* inasmuch as they are freed *from me.*[25]

But if Werner Marx's elaboration of Heideggerian experiences in a non-Heideggerian way is legitimate, then it is appropriate to rethink anxiety in the face of one's mortality as a mood that discloses not only one's freedom but also one's ultimate frailty. Transience, chance, and death permeate all existence. And if this mood makes one aware first of one's dependence on the compassion of others and next of others' dependence on one's own compassion, then conscience calls one to a sense of connectedness and solidarity with others deeper than that of "reciprocal segregation." It is not just that the other faces me as a *free and self-projecting* existence—an end-in-himself whom I have no right to treat solely as a means to my ends and so to whom I am morally liable and accountable. It is also that the other faces me as *thrown* into a situation he can never master: a condition which perpetually reminds him of the vanity of his projects and his effort to take possession of his own life. He sometimes faces me on his knees as an orphan, widow, stranger, or homeless one: a supplicant who depends on me in his hour of need.

John Caputo offers a reading of authenticity that complements Marx's.

> The moral [of Heidegger's hermeneutics] for morals is that none of us occupies a privileged place of insight, none of us has access to a god (or goddess) who passes on to us any hermeneutic secrets. Being nothing more than mortals ourselves, and lacking divine informers, we have little choice but to confess that we do not know the master name.
> "Authenticity" (*Eigentlichkeit*) in radical hermeneutics means owning up to that embarrassment.[26]

But just what is the moral content of this insight into our condition: that every historical epoch, tradition, and perspective not only reveals but also conceals Being, that there is no primordial *ethos*? It is not clear why owning up to the "embarrassment" of our groundlessness—which is an embarrassment only relative to the pretensions of metaphysics—should lead to a morality of compassion rather than to, for example, a cynical relativism or self-assertive individualism.

Caputo assures us, however, that two key virtues follow from authenticity: humility and compassion. First, once one accepts that "we never get the better of the flux, we never make a deep cut into its lethic make-up," one should proceed with caution and *humility* in proposing schemes and programs for dealing with the issues life poses. One should "keep as many options open as possible" and resist the temptation to become dogmatic or fanatical about one's commitments.[27] Second, insofar as authenticity requires owning up to our shortcomings—affirming the limitations and frailties that come with finitude—one should be moved by *compassion* for others who are "siblings of the same flux, brothers and sisters in the same dark night." Again, solitude and solidarity are not opposites, for the solitude into which I am cast when I face my mortality and my responsibility for making something of my own life is precisely what makes possible the insight that "we are a community of mortals bound together by our common fears and lack of metaphysical grounds."[28] And it is important to distinguish the compassion inspired by anxiety in the face of our insecurity from the inauthentic mood of pity.

> Nietzsche condemned pity, for pity is making things easy, refusing to face the worst, throwing metaphysical dust in our eyes, while the truth is difficult. But pity, as Nietzsche himself will grant, is not the same as compassion. Compassion arises precisely from the sense of a common fate, from suffering (*passio*) a common (*com*) comfortlessness. Compassion is the sense of togetherness which mortals share who understand the finitude of the cut they make into things.[29]

Once one gives up the dream of there being absolute foundations on the basis of which one can act—of there being a transcendental high ground or aperspectival view of the whole from which one can speak confidently for "every rational person"—one recognizes, according to Caputo, that the best we can hope for is a humble and compassionate "ethics of otherness" aimed at affirming difference and at providing "the conditions for free and nonmanipulative public debate in which competing viewpoints can be adjudicated."[30] Only an egalitarian community has the right to call itself "true": for only it attests to the "universal" and "legitimate" aspiration of every individual to be included in the common good. Caputo criticizes Heidegger's tendency to find in the Greek city-state an *ethos* more authentic and primordial than our own. Friendship can only be found on a limited scale, and when it forms the basis of political life it is bound to be exclusionary. Women, slaves, and non-Greeks were among those whose voices were silenced in the "brotherhood" of the Athenian polis. True community requires the virtue of civility: a tolerance for dissent and respect for differences among persons who are not necessarily friends.

One does not need the foundationalist moral and political theories of the Enlightenment in order to ground the importance of honoring every person's desire to share in the articulation and enjoyment of the common good. And in fact such theories betray their own ideals when they provide purportedly impartial decision-procedures that would allow someone to speak for what "any rational person" ought to think. Such an impartial judge would have to claim to stand above the interplay of partial perspectives. An egalitarian *ethos* need not be justified on metaphysical grounds, according to Caputo, for acknowledging the moral equality of all persons best reflects the hermeneutic truth that "there is no primordial *ethos*."[31] If we are aware of the contingency of our schemes and that no one has the right to claim access to what is primordial, we should be disposed to give everyone "as big a break as possible" by allowing all—especially those who would likely be oppressed or excluded—to join in the conversation that determines how we wind our way in the darkness.

VII

Whereas a more "Kantian" reading of the meaning of authentic coexistence emphasizes mortality as what discloses a "kingdom of ends" as the regulative ideal implicit in Being-with-Others, a more "Schopenhauerian" reading interprets mortality as disclosing that "we are all siblings of the same flux, brothers and sisters in the same dark night."[32] On the latter interpretation the connection between the authentic individual and others is rooted not primarily in obligation but in compassion. In both cases, however, it is on the basis of an authentic self-relation that one is able to reach out to others as other.

On the "Kantian" reading, exemplified by Sherover, having affirmed myself as a sovereign end-in-itself responsible for my own existence, I concomitantly encounter others as ends-in-themselves, too. Sensitive to the humiliation of being treated by others as mere means, I am aware of the injustice I do to others when I fail to heed the demand addressed to me by the very presence of another transcendence: "Allow me to exist in front of you as your equal!" In calling me to my own freedom, conscience calls me to the freedom of others, too, as a moral dimension of the thrownness which I must confront when I project myself toward my future. My future is always already our future and freedom is always already morally accountable. We are "condemned" to be not only self-responsible but also morally responsible to others.

One can add a "Hegelian" dimension to the "Kantian" reading of Being-in-the-world. If the authentic individual anxiously accepts that existence is unsupported by a timeless ground, he must face up to the partiality and first-personal character of the self-interpretations on the basis of which he decides who he is to be. That one's self-understanding is always prejudiced, however, means not that one should be oblivious to what others think, but rather that one always has something to learn from others, for they may help one to see one's situation in a more whole-minded way. Anxiety reveals not that one's hold on one's own existence should be unaffected by the opinions of others, but instead that one can only know where one stands by engaging in conversation with those who interpret things in other, unexpected ways. The authentic response to the precariousness of one's own perspective on the world is to be responsible to the perspectives of others. The resolve to face "the truth of existence" alone does not imply a dogmatic closure to other points-of-view; rather, it opens one to the plurality of perspectives on our existence given the partiality of any one.

The "Schopenhauerian" reading of authenticity offered by Marx and Caputo gives the movement from self to others a different cast. Having recognized my own vulnerability and need for compassion from others, I am freed from indifference and can turn compassionately toward others as sharers in the same precarious fate. Sensitive to the ways I am taken for granted in the course of everyday life and feeling the preciousness of my own time, I appreciate others not only for their sovereignty but also for the fragility of their efforts to make something of their lives. Aware in my own life that there is not enough time for everything, that time cannot be reversed, and that some losses are irremediable, I am awakened to how precious the goods of life must be from perspectives other than my own. The separateness from "the Others" that I feel in the face of death allows me to feel how essentially I belong to "a community of mortals." The mood that discloses this primordial belonging—compassion—does not need to be secured or grounded from an impersonal point of view. It arises out of, and as a complement to, the very anxiety that attests to the first-personal character of existence.

These alternative "moral" interpretations of authenticity may be complementary; they need not conflict with each other. For both respect for others' freedom and compassion for their suffering follow from an authentic self-relation when such a relation is understood as being an appreciation of both one's capacity for self-determination apart from the "the Anyone" and also one's vulnerability and dependence upon others. The importance of this rethinking of Heidegger's project is that it allows fundamental ontology to "ground" the enlightened, cosmopolitan value of regard for the dignity of all persons—and so defeats worries about the "nihilistic" subjectivism or relativism of hermeneutics—without recourse to an impersonal, rational decision-procedure. It must be maintained that authenticity has a "moral" dimension insofar as the mood which awakens me to the groundlessness and contingency of my own Being-in-the-world also opens me up to others in a new way—so that they are not "given value" in virtue of my own projects or "our" historical self-understanding, but rather make a claim upon and call into question the closure of my or our horizon. Just as the authentic individual is aware of his own Being outside the anonymous sphere of "the Others," so he is attuned to the unique existence of fellow persons outside the horizon of "the Anyone."

But then why doesn't Heidegger say this? Why must our interpretation of authenticity qualify not as a faithful exegesis of Heidegger's text but as a critical elaboration of some understated implications of Heidegger's project—implications that stand in tension with his explicit effort to separate fundamental ontology from morality? Though Heidegger insists that an authentic self-relation enables one to encounter others with a deeper understanding of their "potentiality-for-Being," Gray, Sherover, and Richardson are right to say that he thinks of this as an ontological, not a moral, transformation. Heidegger, we recall from chapter 1, regards morality not as a cure for the ills of inauthentic Being-with-Others but as a symptom of inauthenticity. Moral conscience is "the voice of the Anyone" because it "springs from the limits of the way Dasein interprets itself in falling" (SZ, 294). Even the morally reflective and autonomous individual who has called conventional, public morality into question treats himself as "one-like-others" subject to requirements incumbent on "anyone in my shoes."

The morally conscientious individual, on Heidegger's construal, treats himself as something in the world that can be measured against present-at-hand norms or values. But such an evaluation—in which one "concernfully reckons up 'guilt' and 'innocence,' and balances them off"—presupposes that one has avoided having to choose one's "own-most" possibilities by having opted for possibilities that "have already been decided upon" by reference to an impersonal decision-procedure or table of values. The autonomous individual is inauthentic, according to Heidegger, because he listens to moral conscience "to tell him some-thing useful about assured possibilities for 'taking action' that are avail-able and calculable," and he does this so as to "make certain" that he can account for himself to any rational or responsible person (*SZ*, 294). Rel-ative to existential resolve, moral goodness is "essentially conscienceless" because the person who measures himself against the impartial demands of morality is deaf to the more fundamental demand that he take hold of his own possibilities alone and apart from others: "unsupported by con-cernful solicitude."

Heidegger's mistake in *Being and Time* is to conceive of moral con-science in too limited a fashion. According to Heidegger, the voice of moral conscience is an ontic, not an ontological, phenomenon because it does not open the individual to existence as a whole but rather orients him toward specific possibilities in the everyday world. Moral account-ability allows the individual to bask in "the security of the universal." If moral conscience in the most primordial sense, however, is not the reflective assessment of putative moral truths but rather the acknowl-edgment of a liability antecedently given in the context of one's initial relatedness to the concrete reality of others, then the voice of moral con-science does not play the reassuring role that Heidegger attributes to it. All that moral conscience demands is that one be attentive to the effects of one's decisions on the freedom and well-being of others. This does not necessarily tell one just what to do in any given situation. It simply orients one to a world beyond the immediate horizon of one's own needs, interests, and prejudices. Far from providing possibilities that are "available and calculable," moral conscience has the disruptive and unsettling effect of challenging one's tendency to interpret the world from a self-centered perspective.

That one ought to include the perspectives of others in one's decisions regarding who one is to be does not imply that there is an impersonal, rational decision-procedure allowing one to know what ought to be done. Most of one's responsibilities depend on one's self-chosen ideals. Since there is no one kind of person worth wanting to be, but many spiritual outlooks that are genuinely appealing, many of the things one ought to do depend on first-personal ideals. They are not things that "anyone" ought to do. But there are minimal social require-ments to which anyone is subject on the basis of what one owes to others simply because they are persons. If the moods of respect and compassion alert me to a responsibility I have for others just because they face me as fellow persons, then moral conscience speaks not with the impersonal voice of reason but from the personal stirrings of the affects. Only on the basis of a predeliberative moral orientation toward others does practical reason—the reflective assessment of competing moral considerations and opinions—get a foothold.

Heidegger rejected the conclusion that his "liberal" epigones have drawn from his hermeneutics: that it provides a defense of a democratic, pluralistic, tolerant, conversational culture without grounding these values—or holding that these values need to be grounded—in a transhistorical conception of the good. Heidegger's version of "historicity" led him to attack liberal cosmopolitanism as a symptom of the uprooting, homogenizing force of "technology." John Caputo remarks that Heidegger seems to have been more interested in letting jugs and bridges be than in letting other persons be.[33] Heidegger appears to have thought that an authentic response to our epoch—"the age of the world-picture"—requires the preservation of the vital traditions of local homelands against the leveling tendencies of planetary culture.[34] But *must* the cosmopolitan idea that all persons are moral equals have as its foundation the destruction of a vital *ethos*: the homelessness and homogeneity wrought by "the spirit of objectivity"?

5

"I" and "We": Fundamental Ontology and the Liberalism/Communitarianism Debate

Time and again Heidegger has been accused of failing to do justice to—even of "murdering"—"the other" in *Being and Time*. If Heidegger criticizes the tradition of Western metaphysics for having forgotten the meaning of Being, he is criticized in turn on the grounds that his remembrance of Being remains forgetful of "the other." Fundamental ontology has been condemned for endorsing either egocentricity or relativism. In either case it allegedly traces the moral worth of other persons to the freely constituted projections of the individual or group, and so subverts the commanding authority of others: those to whom one is morally responsible *prior* to one's own or one's community's projections or constructs. Hans Jonas puts the nature of this responsibility in the following way:

> Substantive responsibility concerns not the *ex post facto* determination of what has been done, but the forward determination of what is to be done; by its command, therefore, I feel responsible, not in the first place for my conduct and its consequences but for the *matter* that has a claim on my acting. For example, responsibility for the welfare of oth-

ers does not merely "screen" intended actions with respect to their moral acceptability but obligates to actions not otherwise contemplated at all. Here, the "for" of being responsible is obviously distinct from that in the purely self-related sense. The "what for" lies outside me, but in the effective range of my power, in need of it or threatened by it. It confronts this power of mine with its right-to-be and, through the moral will, enlists it for itself. The matter becomes mine because the power is mine and has a causative relation to just this matter. The dependent in its immanent right becomes commanding, the power in its transitive causality becomes committed, and committed in the double sense of being objectively responsible for what is thus entrusted to it, *and* affectively engaged through the feeling that sides with it, namely, "feeling responsible." In this feeling the abstractly binding finds its concrete tie to the subjective will. This siding of sentiment with the object originates not from the idea of responsibility in general but *from the perceived right-plus-need of the object*, as it affects the sensibility and puts the selfishness of power to shame. First comes the "ought-to-be" of the object, second the ought-to-do of the subject who, in virtue of his power, is called to its care. The demand of the object in the unassuredness of existence, on the one hand, and the conscience of power in the guilt of its causality, on the other hand, conjoin in the affirmative feeling of responsibility on the part of a self that anyway and always must actively encroach on the being of things. If love is also present, then responsibility is inspirited beyond duty by the devotion of the person who learns to tremble for the fate of that which is both worthy of being loved and beloved.[1]

Many of the most prominent interpreters of *Being and Time*— among them Löwith, Buber, and Levinas—have attacked Heidegger for failing to capture an essential mark of our humanity: that freedom is *always already* "invested" with moral responsibility, that the requirement that one treat others with respect—and even a measure of compassion— is not a possible after-effect, but the very condition, of one's own self-responsibility. This implies, as Levinas points out, that moral conscience must be considered an essential structure of Being-in-the-world.

The other is not initially a *fact*, is not an *obstacle*, does not threaten me with death; he is desired in my shame. . . . Conscience welcomes the other. It is the revelation of a resistance to my powers that does not counter them as a greater force, but calls in question the naive right of my powers, my glorious spontaneity as a living being. Morality begins when freedom, instead of being justified by itself, feels itself to be arbitrary and violent.[2]

Moral accountability is a primordial condition of being human that it is up to the individual to own up to; but the individual does not "constitute" *ex novo* the worth of others to whom he is answerable. He can evade the responsibilities that are incumbent on him but he is not free to deny that these obligations have a claim on him and that he can be blamed for violating them. The very fact that the other is a human being imposes obligations that one cannot discount just by detaching oneself from them and refusing to take an interest in them. Insofar as these obligations transcend the "projections" of one's own or one's community's will, they provide a measure against which one is in a position to criticize practices that violate the fundamental principle of respect for all persons.

The issue of whether fundamental ontology is justly convicted of moral nihilism led us to explore three images of authentic existence—the existentialist, the historicist, and the cosmopolitan. I have contended that the cosmopolitan interpretation—which draws out the latent universalistic implications of Heidegger's account of authentic Being-with-Others—answers the charge of moral nihilism to which fundamental ontology is vulnerable when it is interpreted along either existentialist or historicist lines. The cosmopolitan thinker sees his conviction that all persons have dignity and equal moral worth—and therefore that there are certain ways of treating others that are absolutely impermissible—as more than just one local fiction or convention among others. He believes that the statement "Never treat persons solely as means but always also as 'ends-in-themselves'" is a moral *truth*.

But is there justification within fundamental ontology for this cosmopolitan tenet? I have admitted that the cosmopolitan reading requires that Heidegger's thin treatment of authentic Being-with-Others be developed in such a way that it allows for a criticism of his official position that morality is an inauthentic mode of existence. My favored interpretation of authenticity, then, demands that certain underplayed strains in *Being and Time* be accented and turned against the more dominant voices of the text: that, so to speak, Heidegger be read *against* Heidegger.

In chapter 4 we explored different ways of interpreting the claim that an authentic self-relation alters one's ability to respond or be available to other persons: in Heidegger's words, that "Dasein's resoluteness towards itself is what first makes it possible to let the others who are with it 'be' in their ownmost potentiality-for-Being, and to co-disclose this potentiality in the solicitude which leaps forth and liberates" (*SZ*, 298). Insofar as it is the other's existence as a whole to which one becomes attuned on the basis of one's own authenticity, this attunement cannot but have a moral valence. If this revelation of the other person *as* other or Thou is not just an ontological disclosure but the source of a moral imperative, then my awareness of the groundlessness of my own Being-in-the-world is not the basis of existentialist anarchism or historicist relativism. Rather, it provides an experiential basis for the central requirement of a cosmopolitan or universalistic morality: respect for all persons as equal members of "the family of humankind."

And beyond providing the basis for an *obligation* to respect the dignity of others, it can be contended that an authentic relation to one's own fragile finitude allows one to feel *compassion* for others who are acknowledged as "brothers and sisters in the same dark night."[3] Owning up to one's own mortality, on this reading, awakens one from the sleep of indifference to the existence of others that characterizes everyday life first of all and most of the time.

II

The interplay among our three interpretations of the moral significance of authentic existence in *Being and Time* anticipates the contemporary debate between liberals and communitarians over how to construe the relationship between the individual and the community. That debate, too, evolves in three main moments parallelling the existentialist, historicist, and cosmopolitan readings of *Being and Time*: (1) atomistic individualism, (2) communitarianism, and (3) a version of liberalism that answers the communitarian critique of individualism. By exposing a problem that besets the third moment in the liberal/communitarian debate—the attempt to defend liberal values in communitarian terms—we shall be in a position to see how the cosmopolitan interpretation of *Being and Time* faces a similar difficulty; for the claim that all persons are ends-in-themselves and worthy of respect is not obviously compatible with the historicism and antifoundationalism of Heidegger's project.

The authentic individual as portrayed in the existentialist reading of *Being and Time* resembles what Alasdair MacIntyre calls "the emotivist self" and what Michael Sandel labels "the unencumbered self." Of the self as presented by emotivism, MacIntyre writes,

It cannot be simply or unconditionally identified with *any* particular moral attitude or point of view . . . just because of the fact that in the end its judgments are criterionless. . . . Everything may be criticized from whatever standpoint the self has adopted, including the self's choice of standpoint to adopt. . . . This democratized self which has no necessary social content and no necessary social identity can then be anything, can assume any role or take any point of view, because it is in and for itself nothing. . . . The emotivist self can have no rational history in its transitions from one state of moral commitment to another. . . . The self thus conceived, utterly distinct on the one hand from its social embodiments and lacking on the other any rational history of its own, may seem to have a certain abstract and ghostly character.[4]

MacIntyre claims that this self is a "peculiarly modern" phenomenon because its rootlesssness presupposes the loss of "traditional boundaries provided by a social identity and a view of human life as ordered to a given end."[5] What is so morally troubling about this ghostly self is that, if emotivism is true, the crucial distinction between manipulative and nonmanipulative social relations, between treating persons as means and as ends, proves to be illusory. This is because, according to emotivism, "the sole reality of distinctively moral discourse is the attempt of one will to align the attitudes, feelings, preferences and choices of another with its own. Others are always means, never ends."[6]

MacIntyre's "emotivist self" is essentially the same as what Sandel calls "the unencumbered self": a picture of the individual that is "the fullest expression of the Enlightenment's quest for the self-defining subject." To think of the subject as unencumbered

means there is always a distinction between the values I *have* and the person I *am*. To identify any characteristics as *my* aims, ambitions, desires, and so on, is always to imply some subject "me" standing behind them, at a certain distance, and the shape of this "me" must be given prior to any of the aims or attributes I bear. . . . No role or commitment could define me so completely that I could not understand myself without it. No project could be so essential that turning away from it would call into question the person I am. . . . What matters most of all, what is most essential to our personhood, are not the ends we choose but our capacity to choose them. . . . What is denied to the unencumbered self is the possibility of membership in any community bound by moral ties antecedent to choice; he cannot belong to any community where the self *itself* could be at stake. . . . Freed from the dictates of nature and the sanction of social roles, the human subject is installed as sovereign, cast as the author of the only moral meanings there are.[7]

Just as MacIntyre and Sandel point out the morally anarchic consequences of this exaggerated image of a sovereign, self-defining subject, we recall that Marjorie Grene, interpreting *Being and Time* in an existentialist vein, excoriates Heidegger's authentic individual for being unable to encounter others as ends-in-themselves insofar as his care for others refers "essentially and completely to his own free projection of himself." Just as the emotivist or unencumbered self is insensitive to the distinction between manipulative and nonmanipulative social relations, so the authentically free individual "is the man who treats others always as means, never as ends."[8]

In our series of interpretations of *Being and Time*, we saw that an appeal to the cultural and historical situatedness of the self—what we called the "historicist" interpretation of authenticity—is a plausible response to the problems posed by the existentialist version of authentic existence. The historicist argues that the ghostly, abstract image of freedom depicted by the existentialist reading presents a mere caricature of what Heidegger means by authenticity, because the existentialist divorces the individual's free projection of his own existence from his thrownness into a tradition: a communal and historical context which inevitably conditions the way an individual's possibilities open up for him in the first place. Once Heidegger's discussion of Being-unto-death is placed in the more encompassing context of Dasein's "historicality"— once the free projection of one's existence is seen as occurring not in a vacuum but on the basis of possibilities constituted by the heritage to which one *always already belongs*—authenticity cannot be identified with arbitrary self-assertion.

Likewise, communitarians like MacIntyre and Sandel reject the "liberal" interpretation of the person as a sovereign, self-defining subject on the grounds that a person gets moral depth from being governed by commitments that *precede* the willful assertion of an isolated individual. A person is never wholly detached from others but always bears a prior social identity. On Sandel's communitarian interpretation of the relationship between the individual and the community, we cannot view ourselves as existing essentially independent of our aims and attachments

without cost to those loyalties and convictions whose moral force consists partly in the fact that living by them is inseparable from under-

standing ourselves as the particular persons we are—as members of this
family or community or nation or people, as bearers of that history, as
citizens of this republic. Allegiances such as these are more than values
I happen to have, and to hold, at a certain distance. They go beyond
the obligations I voluntarily incur and the "natural duties" I owe to
human beings as such. They allow that to some I owe more than justice
requires or even permits, not by reason of agreements I have made but
instead in virtue of those more or less enduring attachments and commitments that, taken together, partly define the person I am. . . . To
imagine a person incapable of constitutive attachments such as these is
not to conceive an ideally free and rational agent, but to imagine a person wholly without character, without moral depth.[9]

Against "modern individualism," epitomized by the existentialist
movement in philosophy, according to which "the self is detachable
from its social and historical roles and statuses," MacIntyre, like Sandel,
advocates a "narrative view of the self." On the narrative view "the story
of my life is always embedded in the story of those communities from
which I derive my identity." Because I am "constitutively attached" to particular others by virtue of the historically contingent social roles I play,
my good can be understood neither from a universal, impersonal standpoint that would determine what is good for anyone nor from a radically particular—but equally impersonal—standpoint that would construe
the determination of my own good as a groundless assertion of a will in
a social and historical vacuum.

What is good for me has to be what is good for one who inhabits [my]
roles. As such, I inherit from the past of my family, my city, my tribe, my
nation, a variety of debts, inheritances, rightful expectations and obligations. These constitute the givens of my life, my moral starting point.
This is in part what gives my life its own moral particularity.[10]

By situating freedom in a historical and social context, the communitarian restores to the process of self-determination a depth and
content that is absent in the liberal ideal. Likewise, the historicist reading of authenticity in *Being and Time* roots the individual's solitary choice
of himself in the face of death in the wider context of the community
and tradition to which he belongs: a context that lets the individual distinguish between what Bernard Williams calls real and merely notional
possibilities. To say that the individual's choice of who he is to become is
without ground is not to say that "anything goes" but only that there is no

neutral, impersonal language for assessing rival self-interpretations: that the difference between better and worse possibilities is not to be explained by reference to a transcendent third "thing-in-itself" beyond them both. A different way of life or moral system is a real option for us, according to Williams, only if it would be possible for us to adopt it while retaining our "hold on reality" and being able to explain our adoption of it in light of rational comparison between it and the way of life or moral system we now live out. "The life of a Greek Bronze Age chief, or a medieval Samurai, and the outlooks that go with those, are not real options for us: there is no way of living them."[11]

But plenty of morally questionable options—social roles or personal decisions that involve harming others—remain real possibilities for us. Often these options receive the endorsement of at least a segment of the community to which we belong. It is unclear that an appeal to "constitutive attachments" and social roles sanctioned by traditions, institutions, and shared practices gives to self-determination any necessary *moral* content. Why should the good that is a function of the story or stories of which I happen to find myself a part constitute the valid basis of a conception of a *morally* good life? Williams's idea of merely notional possibilities was meant to illustrate the meaning of "relativism at a distance": that the vocabulary of moral appraisal only has a point in relation to the confrontation between real possibilities, that it serves no purpose to condemn the Samurai ideal if this way of life offers no real option for us today. But it is not clear how the communitarian answers the charge of relativism-at-close-hand: the accusation that appealing to one's historically constituted social identity as the basis for one's choice among real possibilities does not offer a sufficiently rational or unprejudiced basis for moral appraisal.

The charge that the communitarian response to liberalism merely replaces a group-centered relativism for individual anarchism—that the emphasis on "constitutive attachments" and "boundaries provided by a social identity and a view of human life as ordered to a given end" threatens those individual rights that limit the authority of the community to impose its vision of the good on persons or groups who beg to differ—parallels the criticism we saw leveled against the historicist interpretation of *Being and Time*. Though the self rooted in a cultural tradition and oriented toward a "communal destiny" possesses more depth than the "radical chooser" depicted by the existentialist interpretation, the historicist interpretation of authenticity invites the charge that it fails to do justice to the individual's fundamental moral responsibilities to other persons. An appeal to tradition as the basis of one's choices leaves one's decisions immune to rational criticism. We recall Ernst Tugendhat's worry that the concept of authentic choice involves a vicious circle when Heidegger tries to give content to the solitary individual's encounter with death by supplementing it with an account of our historical thrownness.

> On the one hand, choice is supposed to free one from the contingencies of the historical possibilities in which one actually finds oneself. On the other hand, choice is rooted in historicity, in the possibilities in which one actually finds oneself. But it is trivial to say that the possibilities to be chosen are those that are in fact given—for this provides no criterion for choice *among* possibilities. Authenticity, therefore, collapses into irrational decision.[12]

Precisely this worry led us to our third interpretation of authenticity: a cosmopolitan reading that emphasized the moral implications of authentic Being-with-Others. And a similar concern motivates an important reply to the communitarians' critique of atomistic individualism. Joel Feinberg worries that MacIntyre's and Sandel's dream of a community in which individuals possess strong social identities because they are bonded by a shared conception of the good requires the repression of persons who do not fit in with the "common good" as it is envisioned by the majority of, or those with the most power in, the community. And the communitarians, according to Feinberg, underestimate the extent to which the pluralistic, liberal tradition—as it is embodied not in the writings of political philosophers but in the societies that protect the political and civil liberties of their members—does not support individual rights at the expense of the common good. Instead, liberalism has its own distinctive conception of the public good consisting in "the harmonious flourishing of diverse groups united by bonds of mutual respect and loyalty to a tradition of tolerance and brotherhood."[13]

Feinberg charges that the communitarians tend to create a false opposition between a coherent, assimilated society with a rich sense of the common good and an atomistic society of isolated individuals who lack any commitment to shared ends. At its best, however, liberalism provides an alternative to the extremes of assimilation and isolation:

> [the] *integration* of individuals into congenial groups that do not smother or trap them, but leave their integrity whole, and their freedom, except for their voluntary commitments, unimpaired. . . . It is less important that we have a strong, comprehensive ideologically uniform

community playing a prominent role in the daily life of its citizens than that we have an abundance of subcommunities that together provide at least *some* place for everyone. The psychological need for a unifying ideology amidst all this healthy diversity would be satisfied by a liberal state built on a creed of mutual tolerance and respect for rights.[14]

Furthermore, the communitarians caricature their opponents in supposing that the liberal's ideology must blind him to the social nature of human beings and the importance to all of us of community membership.

> Liberals may insist, like Mill, that individual self-fulfillment is good for individual human beings, and that personal autonomy is its essential prerequisite. But they can, indeed they must, concede what is plain fact, that most of the things we fulfill when we fulfill ourselves are dispositions implanted by our communities, and most of what we exercise when we exercise our autonomy is what our communities created in us in the first place. Nevertheless, the selves we have inherited in part from these communities are free to select some of their subsequent affiliations and to exercise their autonomy in making new communal commitments, with new consequences for their personal identities.[15]

Feinberg argues that liberalism *can* be reconciled with the social nature of human beings, *can* give weight to the value of fidelity to tradition, *can* do justice to the human need to belong to communities, and *can* honor the importance of civic virtue and public-spiritedness. He concludes that liberalism, properly construed, is not at odds with communitarian thought because "in most of the apparent conflicts between personal autonomy and community, the opposing values can be satisfactorily reconciled, but in the few cases of irreconcilable conflict, it is not implausible to urge that personal autonomy be given priority."[16]

If Feinberg is right, there is no ultimate rift between the self-determination of the individual, the social and historical situatedness within which he exercises his autonomy, and his fundamental moral responsibilities to other persons. This suggests, too, that the cosmopolitan interpretation of *Being and Time*—which takes the historicist reading to task for not doing justice to Dasein's moral obligations to others as "fellow freedoms" or "ends-in-themselves"—need not deny Dasein's rootedness in, and the importance of fidelity to, the traditions of the particular historical community to which he happens to belong. In other words, to affirm that Dasein's self-interpretation is historical through and through is not to deny that one owes others tolerance and respect for their rights.

III

But we must question whether liberalism's discourse of universal rights is actually so consistent with a thoroughgoing communitarianism. And, correspondingly, we must ask whether the cosmopolitan interpretation of authenticity is really compatible with the historicism of *Being and Time.* For isn't the language of human rights, of respect for the inherent dignity and equal moral worth of all persons, of tolerance for diversity, of consideration for persons as ends-in-themselves, a parochial discourse that emerges in one epoch in particular: the Enlightenment? And doesn't the historicist's belief that moralities express the ideals of particular communities under particular historical pressures cut *against* the cosmopolitan notion that some acts are evil wherever and whenever they happen because these acts cause people to suffer what no one should have to endure?

In a perceptive discussion, Evan Simpson defines the main features of the communitarian critique of liberalism: a position he calls "post-modern moral conservatism."[17] This general cast of mind, shared by MacIntyre, Sandel, Oakeshott, Arendt, and Gadamer, among others, claims as one of its key sources Heidegger's "hermeneutic turn." The key lesson of hermeneutics—that there is no neutral metalanguage for assessing rival self-interpretations—is a "*postmodern*" teaching because it presupposes the exhaustion of the "modern," i.e., Enlightenment, project of providing an independent, rational foundation for morality: a principle or system for determining what is good or right that would be accessible to any reasonable individual regardless of his cultural or historical background. The postmodern thinker resists both the ahistorical conception of reason and the atomistic individualism to which Enlightenment "foundationalism" is prone. A person is essentially rooted in a social environment—in a network of relationships, roles, and practices—with its own local, shared conception of the good. And the social environment is a historical phenomenon; there is no ahistorical standpoint from which one can interpret and assess one's social context. Social criticism, therefore, is always context-bound.

It is in this respect that postmodern moral thought is "*conservative.*" Although the social critic must be able to imagine possible ways of being beyond the actually prevailing norms and practices of his society, his imagination is neither free-floating nor guided by a fixed measure. It is instead the envisioning of realistic possibilities with some grounding in the past. Criticism involves the creative appropriation of a heritage to which one already belongs: an appropriation in which one articulates subversive strains in a tradition and turns them against the dominant ones. But criticism is never absolutely revolutionary or *ex nihilo*. If it were it could not make sense to, or have any claim upon, those who are the objects of criticism, for it would be external and not immanent; it would not speak to anything in their lives which they identify as being deficient.

But if one can only criticize the prevailing social and historical order by appealing to reasons that make sense from within the tradition that articulates that order, then it might seem that radical social criticism is impossible. If radical social criticism requires access to standards that wholly transcend the limits of the tradition in which the critic stands and if there is no "higher measure" to which one can appeal, then it would seem that one is destined to conserve the established order. This worry, however, betrays an all too rigid sense of what it means to say that freedom is always rooted in a finite, relative, and historical ground, for the constraints imposed by a tradition do not comprise an inflexible framework but instead allow for a loose and elastic plurality of creative possibilities. There are conflicting voices within any tradition. Social criticism is not a matter of comparing the prevailing ways of thinking with some measure wholly external to them; it is rather a matter of reappropriating the tradition in light of the multiple possibilities it offers and of accenting previously muted or underplayed strains in the polyphony that any rich tradition is. A tradition is not completely closed in on itself. One can still learn from others who differ and from traditions other than one's own. A tradition is always open-ended because the language in which it is couched is capable of hermeneutical enrichment. Its participants are capable of self-questioning in light of new horizons through which their own limits are exposed to them.

Evan Simpson marks out four main features of "post-modern moral conservatism": communal integrity, pluralism, anti-utopianism, and antirationalism. First, according to the communal integrity thesis, each of us bears a historically conditioned social identity that gives his life its moral particularity and conditions what is good for him. Second, there are a plurality of "reasonable" ways of life, spiritual outlooks, or personal ideals, and they are incompatible with any definite list of essential virtues. Codes of moral rectitude are not universal but parochial because local attachments and historical associations permeate our desires and purposes. Third, pluralism should make us wary of the utopianism inherent in any vision of human community that foresees or plans for a final reconciliation of conflicting moralities in a perfect social order. An important consequence of accepting the depth of our historicity is facing the permanence of difference and of conflicting senses of the good and right. Fourth, beyond the general requirements of fairness and utility, rationality underdetermines the complex moral demands that stem from the historically specific relationships defining our social identities.

A crucial issue facing the postmodern moral conservative is relativism: If the right is subordinate to the good, if rights are designed to protect goods immanent in local, shared practices, then how is one to defend the basic "rights of man" that the modern project sought to justify by reference to a universal standard accessible to reason alone or to an essence defining our common humanity? Can one abandon the foundationalist project of modern thought and still defend the liberal political institutions and moral ideals it sought to justify? The worry—which Richard Bernstein calls "Cartesian anxiety"—is that we shall lose confidence in the enlightened ideals of a liberal society if we lose confidence in the foundations that philosophers once hoped would support it: that we need "a permanent, ahistorical matrix or framework to which we can ultimately appeal in determining the nature of rationality, knowledge, reality, truth, goodness, or rightness" if we are to avoid a nihilistic dark age in which rational conversation loses its point because "anything goes."[18]

This anxiety gives rise, according to Simpson, to a *qualified* version of moral conservatism—Feinberg seems to be a case in point—that limits the primacy of local, historically specific conceptions of the good with certain "basic rights" that derive from our "common humanity." These rights set a limit to pluralistic tolerance. Any community that does not honor them cannot claim to possess "integrity" because some of its members are not integrated into the social fabric at all. Universal rights protect the individual against absolutely unjust, provincial conceptions of the good that "shock the conscience of humankind" and practices that violate "the legitimate demands of all humanity on all humanity." Conscience is the faculty by which "any sensible person" knows enough to abhor behavior that violates minimal standards of civility. Basic rights reveal themselves in the recognition that there are some kinds of treatment to which no human being should be subjected, regardless of the prevailing standards and self-interpretation of his or our own society. That we share a common humanity implies that the particular social identity deriving from the group and time to which a person belongs is ultimately trumped by his membership in a cosmopolitan community: a "kingdom of ends" that includes all human beings. But from what standpoint does one claim to have access to a common humanity that transcends time and place? Doesn't this contradict the historicism and pluralism to which moral conservatism is committed? Isn't this defense of liberal culture just the modern, foundationalist project in disguise?

A second version of moral conservatism rejects this "two-tiered," qualified pluralism, but not necessarily the commitment to liberal ideals—so long as we understand this commitment as one that members of *our* culture ought to embrace. The foundationalist's way of appealing to basic rights as a limit to pluralism is to ground them in standards that supposedly do not owe their existence to the historical self-understanding of any particular group. But the discourse of basic human rights is a modern development. It is not a representation of reality as it is "in itself" but rather a pragmatic response to the pressures toward "liberalization" present at a particular time and place. According to Jeffrey Stout, liberal institutions and the moral vocabulary of human rights, respect for the dignity of all persons and tolerance for diversity came into prominence in the eighteenth-century "partly because people recognized putting an end to religious warfare and intolerance as morally good—as rationally preferable to continued attempts at imposing a more nearly complete vision of the good by force."[19] If we come to believe that the moral vocabulary of liberalism based on appeals to our "common humanity" does not have a metaphysical foundation but is, among other things, a pragmatic response to the dangers of religious warfare, should this undermine our confidence in our culture? Does pragmatic historicism warrant "Cartesian anxiety"?

Stout, for one, does not think so. He denies that an antifoundationalist, pragmatic commitment to liberal ideals gives us too little to say in the face of would-be tyrants or deprives us of access to our culture's reservoir of moral reasons. First, even if one could formulate "the" true conception of reason or "the" human essence, this would not subdue the irrational hatreds and resentments that are so often at the heart of the lust to dominate. Second, the pragmatic historicist could draw on the same reasons as the foundationalist in stating his opposition to tyranny. Both could speak of the viciousness of certain kinds of people, the violation of certain rights, the consequences of certain kinds of acts and the relative advantages of a civic life that does not depend on oppression.

If we did not already stand on some common ground we could not even begin to argue. Having assumed or established this common ground, we seek to broaden it, compromise or at least agree to disagree.

Not all judgments are contestable; some form the background of truisms or platitudes without which the conversation could not even get going. But are these judgments then "foundations": unconditioned and absolute? Yes, in the sense that what one could appeal to to justify them would be no more certain than they already are. But no, in the sense that these truisms are not independent of the historically conditioned moral vocabulary in which they are couched. It may be that there are some platitudes without which moral debate could not begin: propositions that must be true insofar as we are capable of moral self-reflection at all. These bedrock truths run deeper than more controversial judgments over which reasonable people may disagree. But it is not the case that these truths are metaphysical for they do not express how things are in themselves independent of our language and social practices.

All that the pragmatic historicist gives up is the foundationalist's dream that the difference between good and evil practices can be explained by reference to a transcendent, third "thing-in-itself" beyond both of them: the vain hope that a conflict of self-interpretations could be settled by reference to a neutral standard of goodness beyond all particular ways of life. The historicist, according to Stout, still has the resources to say that tyranny, slavery, and the torturing of the innocent are really wrong. And he has reason to hold that they are really wrong even if there are cultures that are or would have been justified in believing that these practices are acceptable "given the sorry state of their epistemological and evaluative practices." What we are *justified* in believing about the moral quality of tyranny, slavery, and torture of the innocent "varies according to the evidence and reasoning available to us in our place in culture and history"; but the *truth* of the proposition that they are evil does not vary.[20] Though the endorsement of these practices became blameworthy only when people were in a position to discover what was wrong with them, the practices themselves did not become evil only when they were recognized as such—just as the earth didn't become roundish when people discovered what was right about believing that it is.[21] That we cannot blame those who were justified in believing false propositions given their conceptual scheme or form of life does not imply that we should be skeptical about our own commitments. It only requires that we give up the dream of justifying our moral platitudes by reference to an unconditioned standard that would allow a perfectly impartial judge to distinguish between better and worse options by simply comparing them to the standard: that we accept that there is no access to what is good or right that is not influenced by one's character, culture, and historical location.

Any assessment of competing judgments about what is better or worse expresses the evaluative perspective of the particular language in which the comparison is framed. This perspective conditions what can be said and how different considerations count. To justify one's judgment by appealing to the moral law as it is "in itself" does not explain how the judgment is made and does not help to persuade those who disagree. If good judgment depends not on one's having immediate access to some transcendent moral law but on the practical wisdom gained through education and experience and on beliefs about moral truths that are at most justified in terms that make sense within one's particular cultural horizon, then, in Stout's words, there is no "moral Esperanto": no pure, universal moral language immune to the particularities of one's historical location.[22] But that the liberal vocabulary of human rights, respect for persons, and tolerance for diversity is "the conceptual outgrowth of compromises justified under historical circumstances where people can only secure agreement on a thin conception of the good"[23] by no means implies that those who belong to this culture have any less reason to defend liberal political institutions and moral ideals than they would have if these institutions and ideals had an ahistorical foundation.

The loss of faith in an ahistorical measure against which we could compare our moral truths to see if they are "really" correct should not cause us to lose confidence in our commitments, much less lead us to the conclusion that "anything goes." For the very attempt to stand back from all particular ways of life and moral commitments does not heighten one's understanding of all of them but rather precludes one's understanding any of them. If a person tries in his reflection on the historical relativity of all forms of life to abstract himself totally from the dispositions defining any particular way of living—if he tries to think about himself and the world as if he did not have any predispositions—then he should not be surprised that he cannot find the importance of anything, including the value of his dispositions. This sort of a historicist is really a disappointed foundationalist. He paints himself into an empty corner in which nothing seems to matter because he supposes that if anything were really to matter it would move a "pure" agent—one who begins with no dispositions or prior orientation of concern at all—on the basis of rational considerations alone. In order to judge the worth of any action or practice we must start from where we are—not merely as human or rational beings but as historically situated members of a particular culture with its own ethical language-game and space of relevant considerations.

In a line of argument compatible with Stout's, Charles Taylor contends that the universal attribution of moral personality—the idea that "in fundamental ethical matters, everyone ought to count, and all ought to count in the same way"—represents a basic "*insight*" of Western civilization. It is a "*valid*" idea that "lays obligations on us we cannot ignore": which is to say that one is answerable to the other person as a moral presence whether or not one happens to express an interest in the other. An obligation is categorical if one cannot detach oneself from it and neutralize its goodness just by expressing a sincere lack of interest in it. Yet Taylor admits that the absolute requirement that we "respect other human agents as subjects of practical reasoning on the same footing as ourselves" is a "historically parochial" principle.

> This is not the way the average Greek in ancient times, for instance, looked on his Thracian slave. But, in a sense, it also corresponds to something very deep in human moral reasoning. All moral reasoning is carried on within a community; and it is essential to the very existence of this community that each accord the other interlocutors this status as moral agents. The Greek who may not have accorded it to his Thracian slave most certainly did to his compatriots. That was part and parcel of there being recognized issues of justice between them. What modern civilization has done, partly under the influence of Stoic natural law and Christianity, has been to lift all the parochial restrictions that surrounded this recognition of moral personality in earlier civilizations.[24]

Taylor concludes that the obligation to respect persons just because they are human beings follows from a basic precondition of moral thinking itself—its communal orientation—along with the modern thesis about the racial homogeneity of humanity and the absence of a defensible moral distinction between different classes of human beings: a thesis "which it is pretty hard to challenge in a scientific, de-parochialized and historically sensitive contemporary culture."[25] Taylor would agree with Stout that it might have been "reasonable" within a prescientific, parochial, and historically insensitive culture to have believed in morally relevant distinctions among members of different races or classes and so to have rejected a principle of respect based on the universal attribution of moral personality. And Taylor concurs with Stout that this should not threaten *our* confidence in liberal political practices and moral ideals given the traditions to which we belong. That "radically other" cultural self-understandings can be rational within the horizon of what they take for granted does not give *us* a reason to step back from our own deepest commitments and treat them as arbitrary and merely optional.

Both Stout and Taylor offer the prospect of defending the key principle of cosmopolitan liberalism—the universal attribution of moral personality—not on ahistorical, metaphysical grounds, but rather from within the premises of "post-modern moral conservatism." That they do so does not keep them from holding that this principle is true. All they are saying is that its truth is justified—as are all truths—within a particular tradition: in this case, the tradition which allowed us to see as irrational those who still insist on denying the dignity and moral worth of some human beings on the basis of racial or class distinctions.

IV

The cosmopolitan reading of *Being and Time* invites the charge that it misconstrues fundamental ontology—an account of our Being-in-the-world that appears to support historicism and antifoundationalism in ethics—as laying the *foundation* for an *ahistorical* morality, not unlike Kant's metaphysics of morals. If the cosmopolitan interpretation holds that a proper understanding of authenticity allows us to understand why Dasein is inescapably subject to certain moral responsibilities—obligations that precede one's decision as to how one will take hold of one's own possibilities—this appears to conflict with two basic aspects of Heidegger's vision of the human condition: aspects that would seem to put him at odds with the Enlightenment's project of providing a rational, universally valid foundation for morality.

First, authentic Dasein's anxiety in the face of its own freedom-unto-death is a response to its awareness of the groundlessness of Being-in-the-world and so, it would seem, to the absence of any absolute measure governing one's freedom. Doesn't the claim that Dasein is subject to a categorical imperative to treat other persons as ends and never solely as means imply that Dasein is, after all, subject to an absolute measure? Wouldn't Dasein's recognition of its fundamental moral responsibility to other persons deprive it of the anxiety that comes with believing that its freedom is without an absolute ground?

Second, even if Dasein's choice of itself does not occur in a vacuum—and so is not a creation *ex nihilo*—since one always already bears a historically rooted social identity that allows only some possibilities to emerge as real options within one's actual cultural context, this is not to say that Dasein's resolve has a "foundation" after all, for Dasein's grounds for preferring some possibilities over others are always historically relative—and so not absolute—grounds. Historicality—the structure of Dasein's participation in a larger communal destiny—does not provide a "foundation" for Dasein's choices but only the general context within which Dasein approaches its possibilities. So it would seem that from within the perspective of authentic historicality, the claim that all persons deserve respect because they possess dignity and equal moral worth is at best true-for-us-today, not true simpliciter. Our very capacity to articulate our fundamental obligations in the language of rights presupposes that we belong to the post-Enlightenment period, and this would seem to vitiate the cosmopolitan assertion that authentic existence as such implies regard for all persons as ends-in-themselves.

This sort of historicism calls into question not only claims to moral truth but also the very project of fundamental ontology and the concept of authenticity, however one interprets it. For if Heidegger is true to his historicism, what entitles him to make the ontological/ontic distinction at all? In contending that ontological structures are essential to the meaning of existence is he not purporting to speak truths that transcend the language and epoch in which they are spoken? Is ontology's search for essences compatible with historicism's suspicion that any claim about what is true is rooted in the language-game or conceptual scheme of a particular time and place? The discourse in which Heidegger's articulation of *existentiales* is framed—and the very project of existential phenomenology itself—is a creative continuation of tracks laid down by, among others, Descartes, Kant, Kierkegaard, and Husserl. Though fundamental ontology presents the supposed truth about the structure of human existence, its categories would have been inconceivable in the context of premodern thought. The idea of authenticity, with its emphasis on the self-determination of the solitary individual freed from the traditional boundaries provided by a social identity and a view of human life as ordered to a given end, presupposes the collapse of classical cosmology and Judaeo-Christian theology as metaphysical frameworks that once sought to assure us that our passing lives were part of an enduring, purposive whole. Anxiety articulates a particularly post-Copernican experience of how we are in the world: that we are thrown back on the resources of our own timebound earthliness to make sense of ourselves without recourse to an absolute, "heavenly" measure.

But is fundamental ontology—insofar as it defines historicity as one of the key dimensions of Dasein—deprived of the right to make claims of truth about the experiences and structures it articulates? Mustn't the ontologist suppose that he has a privileged path to things as they really are in order to be warranted in making ontological assertions? Yes and no. Yes, insofar as he claims to be describing the essential structures of Being-in-the-world. But no, in that he need not pretend that his assertions about the nature of existence refer to its Being independent of all language-games and traditions. The ontologist, that is, need not be a metaphysician, if what defines "metaphysics" is the dream of truth as correspondence between what one says about reality and the way things are independent of whatever access to things is provided by language. The pretense of metaphysics is that we could somehow compare how things appear to us with how they are "in themselves," that philosophy can be "a mirror of nature." Heidegger admits that the structures laid out by fundamental ontology only become accessible within a particular interpretive framework. But he denies that "the hermeneutic circle" precludes his making truth-claims about Being-in-the-world. The circle is positive and productive, for Being-in-the-world could only be accessible existentially to one who participates in its structures and the perspectives it affords in the first place.

To say that fundamental ontology is in this sense a historically relative mode of thought does not preclude that it provides us with real insight into the nature of existence. It is just that this insight could not have been expected of thinkers in those epochs ruled by the "onto-theological" idea that human existence has its point in relation to an absolute measure or permanent background-order. It is not only that a proper philosophical account of existence was not accessible to them. It is also that they were not in a position to appropriate their existence authentically, for the very possibility of owning up to existence presupposes, according to Heidegger, the experience of history as the groundless ground of finite Being-in-the-world.

And this circle holds for interpreting the moral dimension of our lives as well. In asserting that all persons are worthy of respect as ends-in-themselves one does not adopt a "view from nowhere." Perhaps the cosmopolitan reading of *Being and Time* conveys the misleading impression that an authentic individual anywhere and at any time would be subject to the obligations stemming from the universal attribution of moral personality. One must give, however, a more historically sensitive version of the cosmopolitan reading by recognizing that fundamental ontology as a whole and authenticity as a personal ideal were not possible within premodern historical horizons. This does not compromise the truth-claims that Heidegger makes about the structure of human existence. It is just to say that this self-understanding would only have been possible given the tradition from which Heidegger writes and, in particular, the historical development Nietzsche called "the death of God."

Likewise, the experience of the other person as one who commands my respect just because he is a human being is only possible given that I can experience my own moral worth not essentially in terms of "my station and its duties"—not in terms of distinctions that are accepted as being given by a natural or divinely authorized order of things—but in virtue of my humanity: that is, my capacity to transcend what is given and appropriate my circumstances freely and creatively. It is not, therefore, that authenticity provides an ahistorical *foundation* for obligations laid upon us by the universal attribution of moral personality, because authenticity is itself a historically conditioned possibility: a self-interpretation accessible to members of a historicized, "postmetaphysical" culture. The point is that given that one honestly faces the *absence* of an absolute measure or permanent background-order securing one's own existence, one cannot but encounter others in a new light.

And it is not that authenticity provides a *rational* basis for morality, for the transformation in the authentic individual's orientation toward others, like the change in his relationship toward his own life, is primarily *affective*. It is not that the authentic individual finds—or needs in the first place—good reasons for being morally answerable to others, but that he faces the other as one toward whom he feels responsible and compassionate in light of the way the other's existence is disclosed to him. In Heidegger's terms, one's anxiety in the face of the groundlessness of one's own existence allows one to "let others be" in accordance with their essential freedom for their own possibilities.

And just as authenticity does not provide a "foundation" for morality, much less a "rational" one, so it does not involve adopting an "*impersonal*" orientation to one's own possibilities. That one's responsibility to others is a prior condition of one's self-responsibility by no means preempts or robs one of anxiety by determining who one is to be in advance according to a neutral standard. For one's moral responsibilities to others underdetermine the existential issue "Who am I to be?" And if authentic moral responsibility involves one's capacity and disposition to pay attention to the other's freedom for *his own* possibilties, then a morally conscientious relationship to the other must be a personal relation to the other in his particularity, not an impersonal relation to the other as an instance of the universal. One way of perhaps inadvertently treating another as a means is to subordinate him to one's own conception of who he should be rather than to pay attention to the uniqueness of his situation as he sees it. The moral relation cannot properly be understood as a species of "the Anyone"; for the impersonality of understanding of what is best for the other in terms of some universal moral principle effaces the first-personal character of the other who is precisely "not just anyone." That one cannot but interpret the other in part by way of "typification" should not obscure the fact that an aspect of attending to the other *as other* is remaining aware of the limits of typification.

This points us back to the key failing in Heidegger's account of existence in *Being and Time*, and reminds us of the respect in which the cosmopolitan interpretation of authenticity is not a faithful reading of the text but requires a supplementation of the structures Heidegger explicitly delineates. For at the beginning of our journey, we saw that Heidegger relegates morality to the domain of inauthenticity because he interprets the voice of moral conscience as a *distraction* from the task of self-responsibility: as a way of *evading* one's particularity by losing oneself in "the security of the universal," in "present-at-hand" norms or values determining what "anyone" ought to do. To approach one's possibilities in moral terms is, according to Heidegger, to orient one's freedom by impersonal, "public" standards rather than to be open to the ultimate privacy and inwardness of freedom-unto-death. I take issue with Heidegger's understanding of the nature of moral conscience. I argue, using Heidegger's own discussion concerning authentic Being-with-Others, that an authentic self-relation can be plausibly interpreted as opening oneself up to the existence of other persons in such a way that one feels responsible for—even compassionate toward—their plight. That one's freedom is always already morally responsible freedom does not imply that one can simply refer to impersonal standards to determine what one ought to do. It only means that one's freedom for one's own possiblities is conditioned by the moral knowledge that one is accountable for the effects of one's choices on the lives of other persons just because they are persons. Once Heidegger's account of human existence is supplemented by a more appropriate interpretation of moral conscience, based on what it means to encounter another authentically, it is clear that fundamental ontology is not guilty of the charge of moral nihilism and that liberal culture can be defended intellectually against the threat of fascism within the limits of the "hermeneutic turn" in philosophy: that is, without recourse to a metaphysical background-order that would provide us with a neutral, ahistorical standard for self-interpretation.

Notes

Introduction

1. Martin Heidegger, "Letter on Humanism," in *Basic Writings*, ed. David Farrell Krell (New York: Harper and Row, 1977), 235.
2. Martin Heidegger, *Being and Time*, trans. John Macquarrie and Edward Robinson (New York: Harper and Row, 1962), 68. All quotations and references to the text will be from this translation. In-text references will hereafter be given as *SZ*, and will be followed by page numbers to the standard German edition of *Sein und Zeit* (Tübingen: Neomarius Verlag, Eighth edition, 1957). These German page numbers are also provided in the margins of the Macquarrie and Robinson translation.
3. Martin Buber, *Between Man and Man*, trans. Ronald Gregor Smith (New York: Macmillan, 1965), xix.
4. Ibid., 174.
5. Stanley Rosen, "Return to the Origin: Reflections on Plato and Contemporary Philosophy," *International Philosophical Quarterly* (Spring 1976), 169.
6. See, e.g., Martin Heidegger, "The Age of the World-Picture," in *The Question concerning Technology*, trans. William Lovitt (New York: Harper Colophon, 1977).
7. Blaise Pascal, *Pensees*, trans. A. J. Krailsheimer (New York: Penguin, 1966), 48.
8. Jürgen Habermas, "Work and *Weltanschauung*: The Heidegger Controversy from a German Perspective," *Critical Inquiry* 15 (Winter 1989), 434.

Chapter 1

1. Many of the categories Heidegger employs are borrowed from Kierkegaard's *The Present Age*, which is not just a description of, but a biting attack on, bourgeois public life in nineteenth-century Christendom for its suppression of "the truth of existence": radical inwardness or subjectivity. But whereas Kierkegaard presents his analysis as a diagnosis of

the spiritual malaise of "the present age," Heidegger goes further in claiming to describe the essence of everyday life everywhere and anytime; his only qualification is that "the extent to which the dominion [of 'the Anyone'] becomes compelling and explicit may change in the course of history" (*SZ*, 129). See Soren Kierkegaard, *The Present Age*, trans. Alexander Dru (New York: Harper and Row, 1962).

2. See Charles Cooley, *Human Nature and Social Order* (New York: Scribner, 1922); David Riesmann, *The Lonely Crowd: A Study of the Changing American Character* (Garden City: Doubleday, 1953); and Christopher Lasch, *The Culture of Narcissism: American Life in an Age of Diminishing Expectations* (New York: Norton, 1978).

3. Hannah Arendt, "Thinking and Moral Considerations," *Social Research* 38, no. 3 (Autumn 1971), 436.

4. Plato, *Gorgias*, trans. Walter Hamilton (London: Penguin, 1960), 76.

5. Michael Walzer, "Notes on Self-Criticism," *Social Research* 54 (1987), 36.

6. On the role of *Besinnung* in the work of Dilthey, see David Carr, *Time, Narrative and History* (Bloomington: Indiana University Press, 1986).

7. Martin Heidegger, *The Basic Problems of Phenomenology*, trans. Albert Hofstadter (Bloomington: Indiana University Press, 1982), 136.

8. Soren Kierkegaard, *Fear and Trembling*, trans. Walter Lowrie (Princeton: Princeton University Press, 1941), 86.

Chapter 2

1. Jean-Paul Sartre, "Existentialism Is a Humanism," in *Existentialism versus Marxism*, ed. George Novack (New York: Delta, 1966), 77–78. Emphasis mine.

2. Richard Rorty, "The Fate of Philosophy," *The New Republic*, 18 October 1982, 33. I have placed Heidegger in the company of the others because Rorty often includes him in the canon of "post-Philosophical" thinkers.

3. Sartre, "Existentialism Is a Humanism," 79.

4. See Charles Taylor, "What Is Human Agency?" in *Human Agency and Language: Philosophical Papers I* (Cambridge: Cambridge University Press, 1985).

5. Ibid., 25.

6. Ibid., 33.

7. Frederic Olafson, *Principles and Persons* (Baltimore: Johns Hopkins University Press, 1967), 107, 164–65.

8. Frederic Olafson, *Ethics and Twentieth-Century Thought* (Englewood Cliffs: Prentice Hall, 1973), 85.

9. Hans Jonas, "Gnosticism, Existentialism and Nihilism," in *The Phenomenon of Life* (New York: Delta, 1968), 228.

10. David Carr, *Time, Narrative and History* (Bloomington: Indiana University Press, 1986), 94.

11. Joseph Fell, *Heidegger and Sartre: An Essay on Being and Place* (New York: Columbia University Press, 1979), 54.

12. Stanley Rosen, *Nihilism* (New Haven: Yale University Press), 142.

13. Iris Murdoch, "Against Dryness: A Polemical Sketch," in *Revisions: Changes Perspectives in Moral Philosophy*, ed. Stanley Hauerwas and Alasdair MacIntyre (Notre Dame: University of Notre Dame Press, 1983), 43.

14. Ibid., 46.

15. See Bernard Williams, *Ethics and the Limits of Philosophy* (Cambridge: Harvard University Press, 1985).

16. Frithjof Bergmann, "The Experiences of Values," in *Revisions: Changing Perspectives in Moral Philosophy*, 141.

17. See Murdoch, "Against Dryness: A Polemical Sketch," 49.

18. For an interesting account of the importance of Weil's thought, see Iris Murdoch, *The Sovereignty of Good* (New York: Schocken, 1970).

19. The formulation in this paragraph of the sense in which Heidegger is attacking the "existentialist" version of nihilism without appealing to an unconditioned, "objective" ground owes a great debt to Joseph Fell's penetrating work, *Heidegger and Sartre*. See especially 115.

20. Ibid.

21. Carr, *Time, Narrative and History*, 56.

Chapter 3

1. Charles Guignon, "Heidegger's 'Authenticity' Revisited," *Review of Metaphysics* 38 (December 1984), 333.

2. Ibid., 337.

3. Charles Guignon, "On Saving Heidegger From Rorty," *Philosophy and Phenomenological Research* 46 (March 1986), 404.

4. Ibid., 405.

5. Ibid.

6. Guignon, "Heidegger's 'Authenticity' Revisited," 338.

7. Philip Rieff, *The Triumph of the Therapeutic: Uses of Faith After Freud* (New York: Harper and Row, 1966), 21.

8. See Emil Fackenheim, *To Mend the World: Foundations of Future Jewish Thought* (New York: Schocken Books, 1982).

9. See Emil Fackenheim, *Metaphysics and Historicity* (Milwaukee: Marquette University Press, 1961).

10. Fackenheim, *To Mend the World*, 153.

11. Ernst Tugendhat, *Self-Consciousness and Self-Determination*, trans. Paul Stern (Cambridge: MIT Press, 1986).

12. Karsten Harries, "Heidegger as a Political Thinker," in *Heidegger and Modern Philosophy*, ed. Michael Murray (New Haven: Yale University Press, 1978), 320.

13. Important contributions to this difficult debate include: Victor Farias, *Heidegger and Nazism*, ed. Paul Burrell (Philadelphia: Temple University Press, 1989); *The Heidegger Controversy*, ed. Richard Wolin (Cambridge: MIT Press, 1993); "Symposium on Heidegger and Nazism," ed. Arnold Davidson, in *Critical Inquiry* 15 (Winter 1989); *The Heidegger Case: On Philosophy and Politics*, ed. Tom Rockmore and Joseph Margolis (Philadelphia: Temple University Press, 1992); and Richard Wolin, *The Politics of Being: The Political Thought of Martin Heidegger* (New York: Columbia University Press, 1990).

14. Heidegger, "The Self-Assertion of the German University: Address Delivered on the Solemn Assumption of the Rectorate of the University of Freiburg," trans. Karsten Harries, *Review of Metaphysics* 38 (1985), 474–75; also see the *Der Spiegel* interview, "Only a God Can Save Us Now," in *The Heidegger Controversy*, ed. Richard Wolin (Cambridge: MIT Press, 1993).

15. Tugendhat, *Self-Consciousness and Self-Determination*, 217.

16. Wolin, *The Politics of Being*, 66.

17. Ibid., 76.

18. Karl Löwith, "My Last Meeting with Heidegger," in *The Heidegger Controversy*, 142.

19. Wolin, *The Politics of Being*, 20.

20. Hannah Arendt, "What is Authority?" in *Between Past and Future* (New York: Viking, 1968), 92.

21. Martin Heidegger, "The Rectorate 1933/34: Facts and Thoughts," trans. Karsten Harries, *Review of Metaphysics* 38 (1985).

Chapter 4

1. Martin Buber, *Between Man and Man*; Karl Löwith, *Nature, History and Existentialism*, trans. Arnold Levinson (Evanston: Northwestern University Press, 1965); Emmanuel Levinas, *Totality and Infinity*, trans. Alphonso Lingis (Pittsburgh: Duquesne University Press, 1969); Michael Theunissen, *The Other: Studies in the Social Ontology of Husserl, Heidegger, Sartre and Buber*, trans. Christopher Macann (Cambridge: MIT Press, 1984).

2. Martin Buber, *The Knowledge of Man*, trans. Maurice Friedman and Ronald Gregor Smith (New York: Harper and Row, 1965).

3. Buber, *Between Man and Man*, 170.

4. Ibid., 82.

5. Marjorie Grene, *Introduction to Existentialism* (Chicago: University of Chicago Press, 1948), 69.

6. Ibid., 70. Emphasis mine.

7. J. Glenn Gray, "Martin Heidegger: On Anticipating My Own Death," *The Personalist* 46 (1965), 447.

8. Frederick Elliston, "Heidegger's Phenomenology of Social Existence," in *Heidegger's Existential Analytic*, ed. Frederick Elliston (New York: Mouton, 1978), 68.

9. William Richardson, "Heidegger and the Quest of Freedom," *Theological Studies* 28 (1967), 296.

10. Ibid., 297.

11. Ibid., 303.

12. Ibid., 297.

13. Hans Jonas, "Heidegger and Theology," in *The Phenomenon of Life* (Chicago: University of Chicago Press, 1966), 258.

14. Charles Sherover, "Founding An Existential Ethic," *Human Studies* 4 (1981), 224.

15. Ibid., 227. Emphasis mine.

16. Ibid., 230.

17. Charles Sherover, "The Political Implications of Heidegger's *Being and Time*: On Blitz's Interpretation," *Interpretation* 12 (1984), 377.

18. Ibid., 378.

19. Ibid., 376.

20. George Schrader, "Responsibility and Existence," in *Existential Phenomenology and Political Theory*, ed. Hwa Yol Jung (Chicago: Regnery, 1972), 288–89.

21. George Schrader, "Autonomy, Heteronomy and Moral Imperatives," *Journal of Philosophy*, 60 (1963), 73.

22. Paul Ricoeur, "A Critique of B. F. Skinner's *Beyond Freedom and Dignity*," in *Social and Political Essays*, trans. David Pellauer (Athens: Ohio University Press, 1974), 63–64.

23. Werner Marx, *Is There a Measure on Earth?: Foundations for a Nonmetaphysical Ethics*, trans. Thomas J. Nenon and Reginald Lilly (Chicago: University of Chicago Press, 1987).

24. Buber, *Between Man and Man*, 170.

25. Theunissen, *The Other*, 191.

26. John Caputo, *Radical Hermeneutics* (Bloomington: Indiana University Press, 1987), 258.

27. Ibid.

28. Ibid., 259.

29. Ibid.

30. Ibid., 261.

31. Ibid., 238.

32. Ibid., 259.

33. Ibid., 266.

34. See especially the 1966 *Der Spiegel* interview, "Only a God Can Save Us Now," trans. David Schendler, *Graduate Faculty Philosophy Journal* 6 (1977).

Chapter 5

1. Hans Jonas, *The Imperative of Responsibility* (Chicago: University of Chicago Press, 1984), 92–93. Emphasis mine.
2. Emmanuel Levinas, *Totality and Infinity*, trans. Alphonso Lingis (Pittsburgh: Duquesne University Press), 84.
3. John Caputo, *Radical Hermeneutics* (Bloomington: Indiana University Press, 1987), 259.
4. Alasdair MacIntyre, *After Virtue* (Notre Dame: University of Notre Dame Press, 1981), 30–31.
5. Ibid., 32.
6. Ibid., 23.
7. Michael Sandel, "The Procedural Republic and the Unencumbered Self," *Political Theory* 12 (1984), 86–87.
8. Marjorie Grene, *Introduction to Existentialism* (Chicago: University of Chicago Press), 70.
9. Sandel, "The Procedural Republic," 90.
10. MacIntyre, *After Virtue* 204–5.
11. Bernard Williams, *Ethics and the Limits of Philosophy* (Cambridge: Harvard University Press, 1985), 182.
12. Ernst Tugendhat, *Self-Consciousness and Self-Determination*, trans. Paul Stern (Cambridge: MIT Press, 1986), 216.
13. Joel Feinberg, "Liberalism, Community and Tradition," *Tikkun* 3 (1988), 40.
14. Ibid., 118.
15. Ibid., 40.
16. Ibid., 39.
17. Evan Simpson, "Moral Conservatism," *Review of Politics* 49 (1987).
18. Richard Bernstein , *Beyond Objectivism and Relativism: Science, Hermeneutics and Praxis* (Philadelphia: University of Pennsylvania Press, 1983), 8.
19. Jeffrey Stout, *Ethics after Babel: The Languages of Morals and Their Discontents* (Boston: Beacon Press, 1988), 212.
20. Ibid., 31.
21. For a more detailed treatment of this issue, see my "Understanding and Blaming: Problems in the Attribution of Moral Responsibility," *Philosophy and Phenomenological Research* 53 (March 1993).
22. Ibid., 286.
23. Ibid., 225.
24. Charles Taylor, "The Diversity of Goods," in *Philosophy and the Human Sciences: Philosophical Papers II* (Cambridge: Cambridge University Press, 1985), 232.
25. Ibid., 241.

Bibliography

Arendt, Hannah. "Martin Heidegger at Eighty." In *Heidegger and Modern Philosophy*, 293–303. Edited by Michael Murray. New Haven: Yale University Press, 1978.

————."Thinking and Moral Considerations." *Social Research* 38, no. 3 (Autumn 1971).

————. "What Is Authority?" In *Between Past and Future*, 91–142. New York: Viking Compass, 1968.

Bergmann, Frithjof. "The Experiences of Values." In *Revisions: Changing Perspectives in Moral Philosophyy*, 127–59. Edited by Stanley Hauerwas and Alasdair MacIntyre. Notre Dame: Notre Dame University Press, 1983.

Bernstein, Richard. *Beyond Objectivism and Relativism: Science, Hermeneutics and Praxis*. Philadelphia: University of Pennsylvania Press, 1983.

Biemel, Walter. *Martin Heidegger: An Illustrated Study*. Translated by J. L. Mehta. New York: Harcourt, Brace, Jovanovich, 1976.

Boelen, Bernard J. "The Question of Ethics in the Thought of Martin Heidegger." In *Heidegger and the Quest for Truth*. Edited by Manfred S. Frings. Chicago: Quadrangle, 1968.

Bouckaert, Luk. "Ontology and Ethics: Reflections on Levinas' Critique of Heidegger." *International Philosophical Quarterly* 10 (1970).

Buber, Martin. *Between Man and Man*. Translated by Ronald Gregor Smith. New York: Macmillan, 1965.

————. *The Knowledge of Man*. Translated by Maurice Friedman and Ronald Gregor Smith. New York: Harper and Row, 1965.

Caputo, John. "Heidegger's Original Ethics." *The New Scholasticism* 45 (1971).

————. *Radical Hermeneutics*. Bloomington: Indiana University Press, 1987.

Carr, David. *Time, Narrative and History*. Bloomington: Indiana University Press, 1986.

Cohen, Richard, editor. *Face-to-Face with Levinas*. Pittsburgh: Duquesne University Press, 1986.

Cooley, Charles. *Human Nature and Social Order*. New York: Scribner, 1922.

Davidson, Arnold I., editor. "Symposium on Heidegger and Nazism." *Critical Inquiry* 15 (Winter 1989).

Dreyfus, Hubert L. and Hall, Harrison, editors. *Heidegger: A Critical Reader*. Oxford: Blackwell, 1992.

Elliston, Frederick. "Heidegger's Phenomenology of Social Existence." In *Heidegger's Existential Analytic.* Edited by Frederick Elliston. New York: Mouton, 1978.

Fackenheim, Emil. *Metaphysics and Historicity.* Milwaukee: Marquette University Press, 1961.

―――. *To Mend the World: Foundations of Future Jewish Thought.* New York: Schocken Books, 1982.

Farias, Victor. *Heidegger and Nazism.* Translated by Paul Burrell. Philadelphia: Temple University Press, 1989.

Feinberg, Joel. "Liberalism, Community and Tradition." *Tikkun* 3 (1988).

Fell, Joseph. *Heidegger and Sartre: An Essay on Being and Place.* New York: Columbia University Press, 1979.

Grant, George Parkin. *English-Speaking Justice.* Notre Dame: Notre Dame University Press, 1985.

―――. "The Morals of Modern Technology." *The Canadian Forum* (October 1986).

Gray, J. Glenn. "Martin Heidegger: On Anticipating My Own Death." *The Personalist* 46 (1965).

Grene, Marjorie. *Introduction to Existentialism.* Chicago: University of Chicago Press, 1948.

Guignon, Charles. *Heidegger and the Problem of Knowledge.* Indianapolis: Hacket Publishing Company, 1983.

―――. "Heidegger's 'Authenticity' Revisited." *Review of Metaphysics* 38 (December 1984).

―――. "On Saving Heideger from Rorty." *Philosophy and Phenomenological Research* 46 (March 1986).

―――, editor. *The Cambridge Companion to Heidegger.* Cambridge: Cambridge Universtiy Press, 1993.

Haar, Michel. "Sartre and Heidegger." In *Jean-Paul Sartre: Contemporary Approaches to His Philosophy.* Edited by Hugh Silverman and Frederick Elliston. Pittsburgh: Duquesne University Press, 1980.

Habermas, Jürgen. "Work and *Weltanschauung*: The Heidegger Controversy from a German Perspective." Translated by John McCumber. *Critical Inquiry* 15 (Winter 1989).

Harries, Karsten. "Fundamental Ontology and the Search for Man's Place." In *Heidegger and Modern Philosophy,* 65–79. Edited by Michael Murray. New Haven: Yale University Press, 1978.

―――. "Heidegger as a Political Thinker." In *Heidegger and Modern Philosophy,* 304–28. Edited by Michael Murray. New Haven: Yale University Press, 1978.

Heidegger, Martin. *The Basic Problems of Phenomenology.* Translated by Albert Hofstadter. Bloomington: Indiana University Press, 1982.

―――. *Basic Writings.* Edited by David Farrell Krell. New York: Harper and Row, 1977.

―――. *Being and Time.* Translated by John Macquarrie and Edward Robinson.

New York: Harper and Row, 1962.

———. "Only a God Can Save Us Now": An Interview with Heidegger from *Der Spiegel.* Translated by David Schendler. *Graduate Faculty Philosophy Journal* 6 (1977).

———. *The Question concerning Technology and Other Essays.* Translated by William Lovitt. New York: Harper, 1977.

———. "The Rectorate 1933/34: Facts and Thoughts." Translated by Karsten Harries. *Review of Metaphysics* 38 (1985).

———. *Sein und Zeit.* Eighth Edition. Tübingen: Max Niemayer Verlag, 1957.

———. "The Self-Assertion of the German University: Address Delivered on the Solemn Assumption of the Rectorate of the University of Freiburg." Translated by Karsten Harries. *Review of Metaphysics* 38 (1985).

Hoy, David Couzens. "History, Historicity and Historiography in *Being and Time.*" In *Heidegger and Modern Philosophy.* Edited by Michael Murray. New Haven: Yale University Press, 1978.

Jonas, Hans. "Gnosticism, Existentialism and Nihilism." In *The Phenomenon of Life,* 211–34. New York: Delta, 1966.

———. "Heidegger and Theology." In *The Phenomenon of Life,* 235–61. New York: Delta, 1966.

———. *The Imperative Of Responsibility.* Chicago: University of Chicago Press, 1984.

Kant, Immanuel. *Foundations of the Metaphysics of Morals.* Translated by Lewis White Beck. Indianapolis: Bobbs-Merrill, 1969.

Kierkegaard, Soren. *Fear and Trembling.* Translated by Walter Lowrie. Princeton: Princeton University Press, 1954.

———. *The Present Age.* Translated by Alexander Dru. New York: Harper and Row, 1962.

Lasch, Christopher. *The Culture of Narcissism: American Life in an Age of Diminishing Expectations.* New York: Norton, 1978.

Levinas, Emmanuel. *Totality and Infinity.* Translated by Alphonso Lingis. Pittsburgh: Duquesne University Press, 1969.

Löwith, Karl. *Nature, History and Existentialism.* Translated by Arnold Levinson. Evanston: Northwestern University Press, 1965.

MacIntyre, Alasdair. *After Virtue.* Notre Dame: University of Notre Dame Press, 1981.

Marx, Werner. *Is There a Measure on Earth?: Foundations for a Nonmetaphysical Ethics.* Translated by Thomas J. Nenon and Reginald Lilly. Chicago: University of Chicago Press, 1987.

Murdoch, Iris. "Against Dryness: A Polemical Sketch." In *Revisions: Changes Perspectives in Moral Philosophy.* Edited by Stanley Hauerwas and Alasdair MacIntyre. Notre Dame: University of Notre Dame Press, 1983.

———. *The Sovereignty of Good over Other Concepts.* New York: Schocken, 1970.

Murray, Michael, editor. *Heidegger and Modern Philosophy.* New Haven: Yale, 1978.

Nietzsche, Friedrich. *Beyond Good and Evil: Prelude to a Philosophy of the Future.*

Translated by Walter Kaufmann. New York: Vintage, 1966.

Olafson, Frederic. *Ethics and Twentieth-Century Thought.* Englewood Cliffs: Prentice Hall, 1973.

———. *Principles and Persons.* Baltimore: Johns Hopkins University Press, 1967.

Plato. *Gorgias.* Translated by W. C. Helmbold. Indianapolis: Bobbs-Merrill, 1952.

Pöggeler, Otto. *Martin Heidegger's Path of Thinking.* Translated by Daniel Magurshak and Samuel Barber. Atlantic Highlands, N.J.: Humanities Press, 1987.

Richardson, William. "Heidegger and the Quest of Freedom." *Theological Studies* 28 (1967).

Ricoeur, Paul. "A Critique of B. F. Skinner's *Beyond Freedom and Dignity.*" In *Social and Political Essays.* Translated by David Pellauer. Athens: Ohio University Press, 1974.

Rieff, Philip. *The Triumph of the Therapeutic: Uses of Faith after Freud.* New York: Harper and Row, 1966.

Riesmann, David. *The Lonely Crowd: A Study of the Changing American Character.* Garden City: Doubleday, 1953.

Rockmore, Thomas and Margolis, Joseph, editors. *The Heidegger Case: Philosophy and Politics.* Philadelphia: Temple University Press, 1992.

Rorty, Richard. "The Fate of Philosophy." *The New Republic,* 18 October 1982.

Rosen, Stanley. *Nihilism.* New Haven: Yale University Press, 1969.

———. "Return to the Origin: Plato and Contemporary Philosophy." *International Philosophical Quarterly* 16 (Spring 1986).

Sandel, Michael. *Liberalism and the Limits of Justice.* Cambridge: Cambridge University Press, 1982.

———. "The Procedural Republic and the Unencumbered Self." *Political Theory* 12 (1984).

Sartre, Jean-Paul. *Being and Nothingness.* Translated by Hazel Barnes. New York: Washington Square Press, 1953.

———. "Existentialism Is a Humanism." In *Existentialism versus Marxism.* Edited by George Novack. New York: Delta, 1966.

Schrader, George. "Autonomy, Heteronomy and Moral Imperatives." *Journal of Philosophy* 60 (1963).

———. "Responsibility and Existence." In *Existential Phenomenology and Political Theory.* Edited by Hwa Yol Jung. Chicago: Regnery, 1972.

Sherover, Charles. "Founding an Existential Ethic." *Human Studies* 4 (1981).

———. "The Political Implications of Heidegger's *Being and Time*: On Blitz's Interpretation." *Interpretation* 12 (1984).

Simpson, Evan. "Moral Conservatism." *Review of Politics* 49 (1987).

Stout, Jeffrey. *Ethics after Babel: The Languages of Morals and Their Discontents.* Boston: Beacon Press, 1988.

Taylor, Charles. "The Diversity of Goods." In *Philosophy and the Human Sciences: Philosophical Papers II.* Cambridge: Cambridge University Press, 1985.

————. "What Is Human Agency?" In *Human Agency and Language: Philosophical Papers II.* Cambridge: Cambridge University Press, 1985

Theunissen, Michael. *The Other: Studies in the Social Ontology of Husserl, Heidegger, Sartre and Buber.* Translated by Christopher Macann. Cambridge: MIT Press, 1984.

Tugendhat, Ernst. *Self-Consciousness and Self-Determination.* Translated by Paul Stern. Cambridge: MIT Press, 1986.

Vogel, Lawrence. "Understanding and Blaming: Problems in the Attribution of Moral Responsibility." *Philosophy and Phenomenological Research* 53 (March 1993).

Walzer, Michael. "Notes on Self-Criticism." *Social Research* 54 (1987).

Williams, Bernard. *Ethics and the Limits of Philosophy.* Cambridge: Harvard University Press, 1985.

Wolin, Richard. *The Politics of Being: The Political Thought of Martin Heidegger.* New York: Columbia University Press, 1990.

————, editor. *The Heidegger Controversy: A Critical Reader.* Cambridge: MIT Press, 1993.

Zimmerman, Michael. *Eclipse of the Self: The Development of Heidegger's Concept of Authenticity.* Athens: Ohio University Press, 1981.

————. *Heidegger's Confrontation with Modernity: Technology, Politics, Art.* Bloomington: Indiana Universtiy Press, 1990.

————. "The Critique of Natural Rights and the Search for a Non-Anthropocentric Basis for Moral Behavior." *Journal of Value Inquiry* 18 (1985).

Index of Names